ALSO BY MARY BUFFETT AND DAVID CLARK

Buffettology

Buffettology Workbook

The New Buffettology

The Tao of Warren Buffett

Warren Buffett and the Interpretation of Financial Statements

Warren Buffett's Management Secrets

WARREN BUFFETT
AND THE ART
OF STOCK ARBITRAGE

Proven Strategies for Arbitrage and
Other Special Investment Situations

MARY BUFFETT & DAVID CLARK

Scribner
NEW YORK LONDON TORONTO SYDNEY

SCRIBNER
A Division of Simon & Schuster, Inc.
1230 Avenue of the Americas
New York, NY 10020

Copyright © 2010 by Mary Buffett and David Clark

First Scribner hardcover edition November 2010

For information about special discounts for bulk purchases, please contact Simon & Schuster Special Sales at 1-866-506-1949 or business@simonandschuster.com.

The Simon & Schuster Speakers Bureau can bring authors to your live event. For more information or to book an event contact the Simon & Schuster Speakers Bureau at 1-866-248-3049 or visit our website at www.simonspeakers.com.

Designed by Kyoko Watanabe
Text set in Sabon

Manufactured in the United States of America

1   3   5   7   9   10   8   6   4   2

ISBN 978-1-4391-9882-7
ISBN 978-1-4516-0645-4 (ebook)

This book is dedicated to the late Benjamin Graham

The man who taught Warren Buffett
the art of stock arbitrage

Give a man a fish and you will feed him for a day. Teach a man to arbitrage and you will feed him forever.

—*Warren Buffett*

CONTENTS

Introduction

One of the great secrets of Warren Buffett's investment success has been his arbitrage and special situations investments. They have been kept out of the public eye, in part, because there has been so little written about them. Also, because brokerage costs that lay investors were forced to pay were often ten to twenty times that of professional investors, arbitrage and special situations have up until now been the sole domain of professional investment trusts and partnerships, who could command much lower brokerage rates.

Previously, brokerages have had two sets of rates: they have had retail rates for lay investors and institutional rates for professional investors. A trade that would cost a retail customer $3,000 might cost an institutional client as little as $150. In the world of arbitrage and special situations, where the per-share profit is often under a dollar, the high retail brokerage rates formed an almost impassable barrier of entry for lay investors, simply because their brokerage costs often exceeded any potential profit in the trade.

In the late 1990s, with the advance of the Internet, brokerages started offering online trading at deep discounts from their full-service retail rates. The absence of a human broker taking the order resulted in greater cost efficiencies, which resulted in the ability to offer individual retail clients lower institutional brokerage rates. With the lower rates the world of stock arbitrage and other special situations suddenly opened up to the masses. Sitting alone with a computer and an online brokerage account with deeply discounted trading rates, an individual investor could compete in the field of arbitrage with even the most powerful of Wall Street firms.

Warren Buffett is probably the greatest player in the arbitrage and special situations game today. Not because he takes the biggest risks. Just the opposite—because he learned how to identify the bet with the least risk, which has enabled him to take very large positions, and produce results that can only be described as spectacular.

In professors Gerald Martin and John Puthenpurackal's study* of Berkshire Hathaway's stock portfolio's performance from 1980 to 2003, they discovered that the portfolio's 261 investments had an average annualized rate of return of 39.3%. Even more amazing was that out of those 261 investments, 59 of them were identified as arbitrage deals. And those 59 arbitrage deals produced an average annualized rate of return of 81.28%! Warren's arbitrage performance not

---

*Professors Martin and Puthenpurackal's study: http://web.archive.org/web/20051104024132 and http://www.fma.org/Chicago/Papers/Imitation_Is_the_Sincerest_Form_of_Flattery.pdf).

only beat his regular portfolio's performance, it also stomped the average annualized performance of every investment operation in America by a mile. No one—be it individual or firm—even came close. (And people wonder how he made so many people millionaires! With such incredible returns how could he not?)

Martin and Puthenpurackal's study also brought to light the powerful influence that Warren's arbitrage operations had on Berkshire's stock portfolio's entire performance. If we cut out Warren's 59 arbitrage investments for that period, we would find that the average annualized return for Berkshire's stock portfolio drops from 39.38% to 26.96%. It was Warren's arbitrage investments that took a great investor and turned him into a worldwide phenomenon.

In 1987, *Forbes* magazine noted that Warren's arbitrage activities earned an amazing 90% that year, while the S&P 500 delivered a miserable 5%. Arbitrage is Warren's secret for producing great results when the rest of the stock market is having a down year.

With Warren's incredible arbitrage performance in mind, and the knowledge that the average investor now has access to institutional brokerage rates, we thought it was high time that we took a serious look at the arbitrage and special situation investment strategies and techniques that produce Warren's mind-numbing results.

Warren Buffett and the Art of Stock Arbitrage is the

first-ever book to explore in detail Warren's world of stock arbitrage and other special situations such as liquidations, spin-offs, and reorganizations. Together we explore how he finds the deals, evaluates them, and makes sure that they are winners. We go into the mathematical equations and intellectual formulas that he uses to determine his projected rate of return, to evaluate risk, and to determine the probability of the deal being a success. In Warren's world, as you will discover, certainty of the deal being completed is everything. We will explain how the high probability of the event happening creates the rare situation in which Warren is willing to use leverage to help boost his performance in these investments to unheard-of numbers.

So without further ado, let's begin our very profitable journey into the world of *Warren Buffett and the Art of Stock Arbitrage.*

MARY BUFFETT AND DAVID CLARK

WARREN BUFFETT
AND THE ART
OF STOCK ARBITRAGE

Overview of Warren's Very Profitable World of Stock Arbitrage and Special Investment Situations

The world of arbitrage and special situations is enormous. It can be found anywhere in the world where commodities, currencies, derivatives, stocks, and bonds are being bought and sold. It is the great equalizer of prices, the reason that gold trades at virtually the same price all over the world; and it is the reason that currency exchange rates stay uniform no matter where our plane lands. A class of investors called arbitrageurs, who make their living practicing the art of arbitrage, are responsible for this.

The classic explanation and example of arbitrage is the London and Paris gold markets, which are both open at the same time during the day. On any given day, if you check the price of gold, you will find that it trades virtually at the same price in both markets, and the reason for this is the arbitrageurs. If gold is trading at $1,200 an ounce on the London market and suddenly spikes up to $1,205 on the Paris market, arbitrageurs will step into the market and buy gold in London for $1,200 an ounce and at the same time sell it in Paris for $1,205 an ounce, locking in as profit the $5 price spread. And arbitrageurs will keep buying and selling until they have either driven the price of gold up in London, or the price down in Paris, to the point that the price spread is gone between the two markets and gold is once again trading at the same price on both the London and Paris exchanges. The arbitrageurs will be pocketing the profits on the price spread between the two markets until the price spread finally disappears. This goes on all day long, every day that the markets are open, year after year, decade after decade, and probably will until the end of time.

Up until the late 1990s the exchange of price information and buying and selling in the different markets was done by telephone, with arbitrageurs screaming orders over the phones at traders on the floors of the different exchanges. Today it is done with high-speed computers and very sophisticated software programs, which are owned and operated by many of the giant financial institutions of the world.

STOCK ARBITRAGE

A very similar phenomenon occurs in the world of stock arbitrage, only instead of arbitraging a price difference between

2

two different markets, we are arbitraging the price difference between what a stock is trading at today versus what someone has offered to buy it from us for on a certain date in the future—usually anywhere from three months to a year out, but the time frame can be longer. The arbitrage opportunity arises when today's market price is lower than the price at which someone's offered to buy it, which lets us make a profit by buying at today's market price and selling in the future at a higher price.

As an example: Company A's stock is trading at $8 a share; Company B comes along and offers to buy Company A for $14 a share in four months. In response to Company B's offer, Company A's stock goes to $12 a share. The simple arbitrage play here would be to buy Company A's stock today at $12 a share and then sell it to Company B in four months for $14 a share, which would give us a $2-a-share profit.

The difference between this and your normal everyday stock investment is that the $14 a share in four months is a solid offer, meaning unless something screws it up, you will be able to sell the stock you paid $12 a share for today for $14 a share in four months. It is this "certainty" of its going up $2 a share in four months that separates it from other investments.

The offer to buy the stock at $14 a share is "certain" because it comes as a legal offer from another business seeking to buy the company. Once the offer is accepted by Company A, it becomes a binding contract between A and B with certain contingencies. The reason that the stock doesn't immediately jump from $8 a share to $14 a share is that there is a risk that the deal might fall apart. In which case we won't be able to sell our stock for $14 a share and A's share price will probably drop back into the neighborhood of $8 a share.

This kind of arbitrage might be thought of as "time arbitrage" in that we are arbitraging two different prices for the company's shares that occur between two points in time, on two very specific dates. This is different from "market" arbitrage where we are arbitraging a price difference between two different markets, usually within minutes of the price discrepancy showing up.

It is this "time" element and the great many variables that come with it that make this kind of arbitrage very difficult to model for computer trading. Instead, it favors hedge fund managers and individual investors like Warren, who are capable of weighing and processing a dozen or more variables, some repetitive, some unique, that can pop up over the period of time the position is held. It is this constant need to monitor the position and interpret the economic environment that brings this kind of arbitrage more within the realm of art than science.

CHAPTER 2

What Creates Warren's
Golden Arbitrage Opportunity

The arbitrage opportunity is created by the price spread between the current market price of the security and its fixed future value. If the future value at some fixed time is greater than the current market price, a positive price spread is created, which can be exploited as an arbitrage opportunity.

There are two reasons for the price spread developing. The first is that every deal has some possibility of not happening. The greater the chance of the deal not happening, the greater the price spread. The less the chance of the deal not happening, the smaller the price spread. A great deal of mental power goes into ascertaining whether or not the deal is going through, and the investing public's perception of the risk involved plays heavily in determining the price spread. As the deal nears completion, the price spread will start to close.

The second reason involves what is called the time value of money. Money, over time, if held in interest-bearing investments, earns more money. So if Company A offers to buy Company B in a year's time for $100 a share, and we spend $100 to buy a share on the day that Company A made the offer, we would be making our $100 back when the deal closed in a year. Doesn't sound too great, does it? In fact, we would also be losing the opportunity cost on the money, since that $100 could have been put to work earning us interest during the year we had it tied up in Company B's stock.

Because of the time value of money, with a cash tender offer, the seller's stock, in theory, will always trade at a value that is slightly less than the value of the buyer's offer. The price spread is at its widest at the beginning and grows closer and closer together as the closing date draws near. If the deal closes in a year, and the offer is for $100 a share, and interest rates are in the 12% range, on the initial date of the offer the stock should trade at a 12% discount to the value of the $100 offer. Then, in theory, each month that passes, as the closing date draws near, the price spread should close by 1% a month, with the price spread between the market price and offer completely closing on the date the deal finally closes.

In Summary

The arbitrage opportunity arises because of a positive price spread that develops between the current market price of the stock and the offering price to buy it in the future. The positive price spread between the two develops because of the risk of the deal falling apart and the time value of money.

CHAPTER 3

Overview of the Different Classes of Arbitrage That Warren Makes Millions Investing In

Historically Warren has focused on seven classes of arbitrage and special situations. In the classic arbitrage category he invests in friendly mergers, hostile takeovers, and corporate tender offers for a company's own stock. In the class of special situations he invests in liquidations, spin-offs, stubs, and reorganizations. Though we will go through each of these classes in great detail later on, it would serve us well to quickly touch on each of them before we delve into their finer points.

FRIENDLY MERGERS

This is where two companies have agreed to merge with each other. An example would be Burlington Northern Santa Fe (BNSF) railway's agreeing to being acquired by Berkshire for $100 a share. This presents an arbitrage opportunity in that BNSF's stock price will trade slightly below Berkshire's offering price, right up until the day the deal closes. These kinds of deals are plentiful and Warren has learned to make a fortune off of them.

Hostile Takeovers

This is where Company A wants to buy Company B, but the management of Company B doesn't want to sell. So Company A decides to make a hostile bid for Company B. Which means that Company A is going to try to buy a controlling interest by taking its offer directly to Company B's shareholders. An example of a hostile takeover would be Kraft Foods Inc.'s hostile takeover bid for Cadbury plc. This kind of corporate battle can get real ugly, but it can offer us lots of opportunity to make a fortune.

Corporate Self-Tender Offers

Sometimes companies will buy back their own shares by purchasing them in the stock market, and sometimes they do it by making a public tender offer directly to their shareholders. An example of this would be Maxgen's tender offer for 6 million of its own shares. Warren has arbitraged a number of these self-tenders in the past and has found them both plentiful and bountiful.

LIQUIDATIONS

This is where a company decides to sell its assets and pay out the proceeds to its shareholders. Sometimes an arbitrage opportunity arises when the price of the company's shares are less than what the liquidated payout will be. An example of this would be when the real estate trust MGI Properties liquidated its portfolio of properties at a higher value than its shares were selling for. It's hard to believe it happened, but it did, and Warren was there.

SPIN-OFFS

Conglomerates often own a collection of a lot of mediocre businesses mixed in with one or two great ones. The mediocre businesses dominate the stock market's valuation of the business as a whole. To realize the true value of the great businesses, the company will sometimes spin them off directly to the shareholders. Warren has figured out that it is possible to buy a great business at a bargain price by buying the conglomerate's shares before the spin-off, as when Dun & Bradstreet spun off Moody's Investors Service.

Spin-offs come under the category of special situations.

Stubs are a special class of financial instrument that represent an interest in some asset of the company. They can also be a minority interest in a company that has been taken private. An arbitrage opportunity arises when the current stub price is lower than the asset value that the stub represents and there is some plan in place to realize the stub's full value. Warren's earliest arbitrage play involved buying shares in a cocoa producer, then trading the shares in for warehouse receipts for actual cocoa, which he then sold. The warehouse receipts were a kind of stub. Though they are known under many different names—minority interests, certificates of beneficial interests, certificates of participation, certificates of contingent interests, warehouse receipts, scrip, and liquidation certificates—they still present us with many wonderful opportunities to profit from them.

REORGANIZATIONS

This is a huge area of special situations that offer some very interesting arbitrage-like opportunities. Warren has invested in a number of these over the years, the most notable being ServiceMaster's conversion from a corporation to a master limited partnership and Tenneco Inc.'s conversion from a corporation into a royalty trust. We will examine his successful investments in both these reorganizations.

Moving Forward

Now that we have briefly outlined some of the different kinds of arbitrage situations that Warren invests in, we need to spend a few pages going over some of the criteria that Warren uses to screen these opportunities for potential returns and probability of success.

CHAPTER 4

Where Warren Begins—the Public Announcement—the Beginning of the Path to Arbitrage Riches

One of the great secrets to Warren's success in the field of arbitrage and other special investment situations is that he will only consider making the investment "after" the deal has been announced to the public.

Understand, there is a whole area of risk arbitrage where money managers stare at their computer screens all day long, trying to figure out which companies will be taken over next so they can invest in them "before" the public announcement. One makes an enormous amount of money, in a very short amount of time, if one has the foresight to invest in the right company, before any announcement that it is going to be taken over.

An example: before Berkshire Hathaway announced that it was buying the Burlington Northern Santa Fe Corporation, BNSF was trading at $76 a share. After Berkshire announced that it was offering to buy BNSF for $100 a share, BNSF's shares jumped to $97 a share. If we had bought BNSF shares for $76 a share and sold them for $97 a share, we would have made a profit of $21 a share, which equates to a rate of return of approximately 27% on our investment. Not too shabby. But to earn that 27% we would have had to be either very lucky or blessed with the foresight to see it coming. And few people have that kind of foresight; mostly they are just trading on rumors and tidbits of inside information.

Warren isn't interested in trading on rumors or inside information. For Warren a very iffy $21-a-share profit is not as good as an absolutely certain $3-a-share profit, which is what he would have made had he arbitraged Berkshire's buyout of BNSF at $97 a share ($100 – $97 = $3). It may not seem like much, but the certainty of the deal allows him a quick and certain return and the prospect of using great amounts of leverage to more than triple his initial rate of return on his real out-of-pocket cost. It is the "certainty" that allows him to be comfortable leveraging up on the transaction. And it is leverage that adds rocket juice to his return. We'll get more into the power of leverage in arbitrage situations later on.

Risk Arbitrage

But to better understand Warren's unique perspective on arbitrage we should spend a moment talking about the negative aspects of risk arbitrage as it is practiced on Wall Street and how that contrasts with Warren's strategy.

The world of risk arbitrage is enormous, with most large-scale Wall Street risk arbitrage operations having as many as fifty potential deals going on at once. They operate on the theory that if most of the deals go bad, the few winners will more than make up for the losses. However, a large-risk operation requires a constant monitoring of fifty or more positions, which means reading the financial press and SEC filings for fifty or more deals. Besides being an enormous amount of work, the great number of positions also escalates the probability of error. And error, in the risk arbitrage game, is what can lose us serious money.

WARREN'S PERSPECTIVE

Warren has discovered that the secret to consistently winning in the arbitrage game is to concentrate on just a few deals that have a high probability or "certainty" of being completed. Through careful analysis before he goes in and by keeping a watchful eye on the deal after he invests, he can confidently take significant positions, which can produce meaningful results.

While this affords Warren the possibility of great financial gain, it also presents the potential for significant loss. The potential for loss occurs when the deal falls apart. This can send security prices back to their pre-announced deal status, which is usually much lower than the price he paid after the deal was announced. This is why Warren has to be as close as he can be to "absolutely certain" that the deal will reach fruition, because if he isn't, he could end up losing a bundle.

In Summary

Warren is only interested in investing in deals that he is certain will be completed. He is not a man who plays in the gray areas of arbitrage or other special situations; he leaves those to the speculators. He is about making sure the event will occur within the time frame he is predicting it will. It is the certainty of the deal that reduces the risk and allows him to take meaningful positions that can result in superior results.

CHAPTER 5

The Arbitrage Risk Equation Warren Learned from Benjamin Graham and How It Can Help Make Us Rich

Benjamin Graham, Warren's teacher, mentor, and friend, taught him an arbitrage risk equation that adjusts the potential return of the deal with the probability of its happening. This gives him a risk-adjusted potential rate of return on the investment.

While we can be sure that Warren followed Graham's procedure in his early years, it is questionable whether he still does. More likely than not, Warren quickly runs through his criteria for determining the "certainty" of the deal and whether or not it offers an attractive return. Warren stays away from the gray areas with almost all his investments, keeping to what he knows and what he is sure of. If we have to run a risk calculation to know whether or not we should be in the deal, then the deal probably falls into the gray areas of "certainty" and should be avoided.

However, for the sake of our own education, we thought

we would include the Graham risk equation. Having to run this risk equation in the beginning of our career as an arbitrage investor helps us acquire the discipline to always review all the different variables that help to determine the "certainty" of the deal.

The first part of the equation requires that we determine what our potential return is. To do this we take the amount we expect to earn from the transaction, be it a tender offer, liquidation, reorganization, or other event, and divide it by the amount of our investment. Let's say the tender offer is for $55 a share and we can buy the stock at $50 a share. This means our arbitrage investment has a projected profit (PP) of $5 a share on our investment (I) of $50 a share ($55 − $50 = $5). This gives us a 10% projected rate of return (PRR) on our $50 investment ($5 ÷ $50 = 10%).

$$\text{PP (\$5)} \div \text{I (\$50)} = \text{PRR (10\%)}$$

The next thing we have to do is figure out the likelihood that the event will occur as a percentage. Does it have a 30% chance of being completed? Or a 90% chance? Which means we have to go through the different variables we discussed throughout this book, weigh them in relation to the success of the deal, and come up with a percentage chance of the deal being done. There is no set calculation for doing this; it is a learned art that comes with experience. The more experience you get, the better you get at weighing the different variables and coming up with a percentage chance that the deal will be completed, which we will label the likelihood of the deal happening, or LDH.

The next thing we do is to take the likelihood of the deal happening (LDH) and multiply it by the projected profit (PP), which gives us the adjusted projected profit (APP).

A $5 projected profit (PP) multiplied by a 90% likelihood of the deal happening (LDH) equates to an adjusted projected profit (APP) of $4.50 ($5 x 0.9 = $4.50).

Adjustment equation: PP ($5) x LDH (90%) = APP ($4.50)

We can then calculate our adjusted projected rate of return (APRR) by taking our projected profit (PP) and dividing it by our investment (I) of $50 a share, which will give us an APRR of 9% ($4.50 ÷ $50 = 0.09).

PP ($4.50) ÷ I ($50) = APRR (9%)

Now that we know our adjusted projected profit ($4.50) and our adjusted projected rate of return (9%), we need to factor in the risk of the deal falling apart. If the deal fails to be completed, we will assume that the per-share price of the stock will return to the trading price it had before the tender offer was announced. We will call this part of the equation the projected loss, which calculates our risk of loss. As an example: If the stock was trading at $44 a share before the announcement of the $55-a-share tender offer and after the announcement that we are buying the stock at $50 a share, we have a downside risk of $6 a share if the deal falls apart and the price of the company's stock returns to $44 a share ($50 – $44 = $6). Thus, if the deal falls apart, we have a projected loss (PL) of $6 a share.

But since we have projected that there is a 90% likelihood of the deal happening, there is only a 10% chance of the deal falling apart and us losing $6 a share. We will call this the likelihood of the deal falling apart (LDFA), which in this example is equal to 10%.

Next we take the projected loss (PL) of $6 a share and multiply it by the 10% likelihood of the deal falling apart (LDFA), which gives us an adjusted projected loss (APL) of $0.60 a share ($6 x 0.1 = $0.60).

PL ($6) x LDFA (10%) = APL ($0.60)

Now the number we are really after is our risk-adjusted projected profit (RAPP), which, in turn, will also give us our risk-adjusted projected rate of return (RAPRR). To find the risk-adjusted projected rate of return (RAPRR), we take our adjusted potential profit (APP) of $4.50 a share and subtract from it our adjusted projected loss (APL) of $0.60 a share. This gives us a risk-adjusted projected profit (RAPP) of $3.90 a share ($4.50 − $0.60 = $3.90).

APP ($4.50) − APL ($0.60) = RAPP ($3.90)

If we take the risk-adjusted projected profit (RAPP) of $3.90 and divide it by our investment (I) of $50 a share, we get a risk-adjusted projected rate of return (RAPRR) on our investment of 7.8% ($3.90 ÷ $50 = 0.078).

RAPP ($3.90) ÷ I ($50) = RAPRR (7.8%)

The question then becomes is a risk-adjusted projected rate of return of 7.8% an enticing enough return for us? If it is, we make our investment. Understand that in using this equation it is possible to produce negative numbers. In the prior example, if our adjusted projected loss (APL) had been $7 instead of $0.60, then our risk-adjusted projected profit (RAPP) would be −$2.50 a share ($4.50 − $7 = −$2.50). And under the investment rules for using this equation, if the risk-adjusted projected profit (RAPP) is a negative number, we walk from the deal.

In Summary

While it is fun to ponder the different variables in assessing the risk in any arbitrage deal, calculations should only serve as a means to help us think about the potential of the opportunity presented. At the end of the day, running a successful arbitrage operation has more to do with the art of weighing the different variables than attempting to quantify them down to a hard scientific equation that tells us when to buy and when to sell. The reason for this is that the variables themselves can change, and often they are simply unique to that situation. And as Warren always warns, "Beware of Geeks bearing numbers." Still, they are tools, and they are tools that can be helpful if used properly.

CHAPTER 6

How Warren Uses the Annual Rate of Return to Determine the Investment's Attractiveness

The funny thing about stock arbitrage and other special investment situations is that a 5% return may end up being a better deal than a 20% return. (That should get your attention!) The reason for this is that the time it takes to close the merger, do the liquidation, execute the spin-off, or reorganize the company plays a huge part in determining our annual rate of return and the overall attractiveness of the investment.

Let's work with an example: if one is able to get a 5% return in a month, we could argue that it is a better investment than one that earns us a 20% return over a two-year period. And the reason for this is that a 5% rate of return in a month is arguably the equivalent of getting a yearly rate of return of 60% (0.05 x 12 = 0.6). Which is what it would take to produce a monthly rate of return of 5%.

Likewise, a 20% return at the end of two years is arguably the same as only getting a 10% yearly rate of return (0.2 ÷ 2 years = 0.1).

Of course, this argument is premised on being able to reallocate the capital that we had out at 5% for a month, at attractive rates in the preceding months. But in theory, if you could reallocate your capital five times over a two-year period and each time earn 5% a month, it would still produce better results than getting a 20% return at the end of a two-year period.

Both Warren and Graham viewed the investment worthiness of an arbitrage or special situation investment from the perspective of a yearly or annual rate of return, because it gave them a basis for comparing it to other investment opportunities, which are almost always quoted in yearly terms. Even our local banks quote us three- and six-month CDs in yearly terms. The year is the base time standard by which Warren compares different investment returns.

Thus, the rule is this: the time it takes to achieve the projected profit ultimately determines a great deal of the investment's attractiveness. So, in determining the worthiness of an arbitrage or other special situation investment, we always adjust the return to put it into a yearly perspective.

THE CALCULATION

The calculation that Warren uses takes the projected profit and divides it by the amount invested. A projected profit of

$10 a share on an investment of $100 per share equates to a 10% rate of return (10 ÷ 100 = 0.1). The rate of return is then divided by the number of months we project it will take to earn that rate of return. If it takes ten months to earn a 10% rate of return, then we would divide the 10% rate of return by 10, which would give us a monthly non-compounding rate of return of 1%, which we would then multiply by 12, which would tell us that our 10% rate of return over a ten-month period equates to an annual rate of return of 12%.

To determine an annual rate of return on a projected rate of return of 25% over a period in excess of a year, say eighteen months, we would take the 25% rate of return and divide it by 18, which would give us a monthly rate of return of 1.3% (.25 ÷ 18 = .013). We would then multiply our monthly return of 1.3% by 12 (number of months in one year), and we would get a projected annual rate of return of 15.6% (.013 x 12 = .156).

Thus, the variables are:

Projected Rate of Return = PRR
Number of Months = NM
Monthly Rate of Return = MRR
Months in Year = MY
Annual Rate of Return = ARR

The equations using the above example are:

PRR ÷ NM = MRR

MMR x MY = ARR

As applied to the above examples:

PRR (0.1) ÷ NM (10) = MRR (0.01)

MMR (0.01) x MY (12) = ARR (0.12)

And

PRR (0.25) ÷ NM (18) = MRR (0.013)

MMR (0.013) x MY (12) = ARR (0.156)

In Summary

The lesson here is that the time it takes to get to fruition ultimately determines our annual rate of return. In fact, time ultimately determines the attractiveness of the deal. Both Warren and Graham like to view arbitrage and special situation returns from a yearly perspective, which makes it possible to put them into perspective compared to what other investments are paying.

CHAPTER 7

Leverage and Arbitrage—How Warren Uses Borrowed Money to Triple His Returns

From Warren's perspective the certainty of the deal presents him with an opportunity to safely use leverage—borrowed money—to increase his rate of return. Though Warren has long spoken against the evils of borrowing money to buy stocks, with arbitrage situations that he is certain will reach fruition he is willing to make an exception. And he has done so since the early days of the Buffett Investment Partnership.

Let us explain the dynamics of Warren's arbitrage strategy and how it enables him to safely use large amounts of leverage. The danger with any stock investment is that it will not perform, that the share price won't increase, that it will drop like a rock, taking our capital with it. Borrowing money to invest in a risky investment is a sure way to eventually go broke.

What Warren has discovered is that a high probability of the arbitrage deal being completed equates to a large amount of the risk being removed. Not that we can ever remove all the risk, but if most of it is removed, then most of the risk of using borrowed money is also removed. It is the certainty of the arbitrage deal that allows him to use large amounts of leverage.

Basically, Warren has figured out that if he is "certain" that he is going to make his projected profit, it is safe to use borrowed money to increase his rate of return.

THE POWER OF LEVERAGE

To better understand the power of leverage it is best to run through a quick deal. Imagine that Corporation A offers to buy Corporation B for $50 a share. Corp. B agrees to the price, and this friendly merger is expected to close in six months.

Immediately after the public announcement of the friendly merger between the two companies, Corp. B's shares are trading at around $48 a share. Which means that if we bought Corp. B's shares at $48 a share and in six months sold them to Corp. A for $50 a share, when the merger closed, we would make $2 a share, which equates to a 4% return for the six months we held the investment. A 4% return in six months equates to an annual rate of return of 8%.

Now, where it gets really interesting is if we add leverage to the equation: if we had borrowed the $48 at an annual rate of 6%, which equates to a 3% rate of interest for the six-month period, we could calculate our interest costs at $1.44 a share ($48 x 0.03 = $1.44). With an interest cost of $1.44, and a profit potential of $2 a share, we can calculate a projected profit of $0.56 a share ($2 – $1.44 = $0.56).

Now our cost of a share of B's stock is $48, but we are borrowing the $48 at an interest cost of $1.44. So our real investment cost is $1.44 a share, provided that the investment works out. Now if we earn $0.56 a share, on an investment of $1.44, our return will be 38% ($0.56 ÷ $1.44 = 0.38) for the six month period, which equates to earning an annual rate of return of 76%.

Invest our own $48 and earn 4% or borrow the $48 at a cost of $1.44 in interest and earn a 38% return. Which one looks more enticing? Yes, borrowing the money gives us tremendous leverage, which greatly increases our return. However, it also greatly increases the risk in the deal. What Warren discovered is that the certainty of the deal—the high probability of its success—counterbalances the risk added by the use of leverage. It is the "certainty" of the deal that makes using borrowed money both safe and smart.

Borrowing the Money

Borrowing the money to invest in arbitrage situations is as easy as calling our broker and arranging a margin account.

Basically we can borrow up to 50% on the securities that we are buying. We can also borrow against stocks we already own. So if we have a $100,000 portfolio of stocks, we can go and borrow another $100,000. (The original $100,000 in our portfolio gives us the collateral to borrow our first $50,000 and the newly purchased shares will provide us with collateral for the second $50,000.)

Thus, if we have a $50 million portfolio, we can borrow another $50 million. Which is what Warren did in his early years to help him produce all those winning years for the Buffett Partnership. When the rest of the market was taking a nosedive, he leveraged up on the arbitrage deals and made fantastic returns, which countered the effects of a poor performance in the rest of the partnership's portfolio. Leveraging up in arbitrage situations allowed him to pull the proverbial rabbit out of the hat time and time again. (Note that during the Buffett Partnership years he set a limit on borrowed money for arbitrage deals to 25% of the value of the partnership's net worth. He wrote in his 1963 annual letter to his partners, "I believe in using borrowed money to offset a portion of our arbitrage portfolio, since there is a high degree of safety in this category in terms of both eventual results and intermediate market behavior. . . . My self-imposed standard limit regarding borrowing is 25% of partnership net worth, although something extraordinary could result in modifying this for a limited period of time." We might be wise to follow in Warren's limitation for using leverage in our own portfolio of arbitrage deals.)

THE TIME DANGER OF USING LEVERAGE

The use of leverage gives Warren the advantage of being able to pull additional earning power out of capital tied up in other investments. Why doesn't Warren use leverage with all his other stock investments? There are two reasons: (1) If the deal or event that drives the profit isn't certain, then borrowing capital to invest in it can be an invitation to folly, and (2) If the time element is not certain, then determining the difference between the cost of borrowed capital and the rate of return becomes an impossible calculation.

As an example: let's say that we borrow $1 million at 5% a year to invest in a stock that we are projecting will earn us $150,000 after holding it for a year. This means that we will earn a gross return of $150,000, less our interest costs of $50,000, which leaves us with a profit of $100,000 ($150,000 − $50,000 = $100,000). So let's say we make the investment, but instead of its taking one year for our stock to move up, it takes four years. The borrowed money is costing us $50,000 a year, so if it we hold it for four years, our interest costs will balloon to $200,000. Which means that even if the deal comes through and we gross $150,000, we still end up losing $50,000 ($150,000 − $200,000 = $50,000). In the game of using leverage, time is never on our side—quicker is always better.

But we can comfortably borrow $1 million at 5% to invest if we are "certain" that the deal will be completed in the time period we projected. It is the "certainty" of both the time and the return that allows Warren to leverage up and use borrowed money to safely invest in arbitrage and other special situations.

In Summary

Leveraging up for arbitrage deals and other special situations was the way that Warren pulled greater earning power out of the Buffett Partnership's underlying stock portfolio. It is also a technique that he used often during his first twenty years at the helm of Berkshire to improve the overall performance of Berkshire's portfolio. If used carefully, and only with deals where there is a high probability of performance, this strategy makes it possible to greatly enhance the performance of our arbitrage investments.

THE ARBITRAGE AND
SPECIAL SITUATION DEALS

CHAPTER 8

Overview of Mergers and Acquisitions—Where Warren Has Made Millions

Mergers and acquisitions is the area of finance that has presented Warren the greatest opportunity to profit from arbitrage situations. Of all the arbitrage deals, these are the most garden variety, the easiest to identify, and the easiest to follow. Large corporations have long ago figured out that if they are going to grow, they are going to have to either merge with or acquire other businesses. And when they do they are most happy to announce to the world their intentions, and the financial press is equally happy to follow their progress. As entire industries continue to consolidate—be they pharmaceutical, chemical, food, petroleum, railroad, or financial—this area of finance will continue to supply us with many golden arbitrage opportunities to ply our trade.

The words "merger" and "acquisition" are often used interchangeably—but for our purposes they have two distinct differences. The ability to recognize these differences will help us select the procedure we will use in determining their investment worthiness.

In a merger, two or more companies must actively agree to join together as a single entity. A merger usually requires the approval of the shareholders of the companies that are merging together.

An acquisition can be completed with the sole actions of a single company, and the acquisition of the target company can be hostile—meaning done without the consent of the board of the company it is seeking to acquire. The company can go into the market and buy control in the business without anyone's approval and then replace the board of the target company with directors of its choosing.

With these differences in mind, let's look at each one separately, identifying, as we go along, the moneymaking arbitrage opportunities they offer us.

CHAPTER 9

Friendly Mergers—Warren's Favorite Arbitrage Investment

In a merger, two companies agree to join together to form a single business entity. However, even though it is a friendly merger, one of the combining companies will become the dominant operating business. The other business, the subdominant company, is folded into the dominant company. The arbitrage opportunity lies in the securities of subdominant companies, the ones merging with the dominant ones.

The first thing we have to do when assessing a merger between two companies is to determine which is the dominant one and which is the subdominant one. This is easy to do—the dominant one is the entity that is offering to exchange its cash or shares or both for the other company's shares. Think of it as one company swallowing the other company. We want to own the company that is being swallowed. In the recent Berkshire Hathaway merger with BNSF railroad, Berkshire was the dominant company and BNSF the subdominant one. If we were arbitraging this merger, we would have bought BNSF's stock.

After we have identified the dominant and subdominant companies, we need to figure out the terms of the deal. Is the dominant company trading its shares for the subdominant company's shares? Or is it the dominant company trading its cash and shares for the subdominant company's shares? Or is it the dominant company trading just its cash for the subdominant company's shares?

SHARES-FOR-SHARES EXAMPLE

Company A and Company B have agreed to merge. The closing date is in six months. In the deal, Company A has offered 2.5 shares of its stock for every one share of Company B's stock. This means that at the closing Company A will exchange 2.5 shares of its stock for every share of Company B we own.

Trying to arbitrage a stock-for-stock deal may seem complicated, but actually it is quite easy. You take the price of a share of Company A's stock and multiply it by the 2.5 share offer and then subtract it from the price of a share of Company's B's stock. If the difference is positive, you have an arbitrage opportunity. So, if Company A's stock is trading at $23 a share and Company B's is trading at $45 a share, we would multiply $23 by 2.5, which would give us a value of $57.50 for Company A's 2.5 shares ($23 x 2.5 = $57.50). Subtract $45, the price of a single share of Company B, from $57.50 and you get a profit on the deal of $12.50 a share ($57.50 – $45 = $12.50).

The next move is to lock in the profit. The reason we lock in the profit rather than wait for the actual closing date is that "all stock" deals will often see the price spread between the two companies diminish as the closing date approaches. This can work against us. In a situation where the trading price of Company A's stock diminishes, Company A's 2.5 share offer may be worth less than $57.50 at the time of close, which means we pay $45 for a share of Company B but get 2.5 shares of Company A that are worth, say, $54. Because of fluctuating market values it is best to lock in the profit.

To lock in our profit we would buy one share of Company B and short 2.5 shares of Company A's stock. Then, on the closing date of the merger, we would exchange our one share of Company B stock for 2.5 shares of Company A stock. We would then take the 2.5 shares of Company A's stock we got in the exchange and use them to close out our Company A short position.

It's that easy.

STOCK AND CASH DEAL

In a stock and cash deal we only have to worry about locking in the stock portion of the deal, as the shares can fluctuate in value and change the attractiveness of the deal. The cash portion won't change and will be tendered at close.

As an example: in a stock and cash deal where Company A's stock is trading at $23 a share and Company B's stock is trading at $43 a share, Company A might offer two shares of its stock and $11.50 in cash for one share of Company B's stock, for a total value of $57.50. In this case, if we wanted to lock in the profit, we would buy a share of Company B, and short the two shares of Company A. Then, at the close of the deal, we would exchange our one share of Company B for two shares of Company A and $11.50 in cash. Then we would use the two shares of Company A to close out the short position in Company A.

PURE CASH DEAL

If the merger is 100% in cash, we needn't worry about locking in the profit, as it is fixed by the terms of the merger agreement and cash doesn't fluctuate in value.

As an example: in a pure cash deal Company A would be offering $57.50 in cash for a share of Company B. Here we would subtract the per-share price of a share of Company B's stock, $45, from Company A's offer of $57.50, to determine our profit, which would be $12.50. Since Company A is going to tender $57.50 in cash at the close, there is no need to lock in the spread. In fact, Company A's market price is of no concern to us; it can go up and down all it wants and not affect the results of our arbitrage position. As soon as we bought a share of Company B our profit was locked in. The only catch is we have to wait till the closing of the deal to get our money.

Note: a day or two before the closing of the deal, the market will often fully price Company B's shares at or very close to the deal price, and some arbitrageurs prefer to liquidate the position by selling out directly to the market. They do this for two reasons: (1) Sometimes deals fall apart at the very end; and (2) Sometimes it can take the dominant company three to four weeks to get us our money. Nobody likes waiting to get their money.

A Stock-for-Stock Deal with a Guaranteed Value

A variation on a stock-for-stock deal is for the dominant company to guarantee a set value for the subdominant company's shares. Company A promises to tender $57 worth of its shares at closing for each share of Company B. This effectively stops the short selling of Company A's shares, because the value is locked in by a set value quoted in dollars.

To value one of these deals, we would subtract the price of a share of Company B from the $57, which would give us our projected profit on the deal. So if a share of B's stock is selling at $55 a share and the deal promises the equivalent value of $57 a share in A's stock, we would calculate our profit by subtracting $55 from $57 and get a profit of $2 a share ($57 – $55 = $2).

Setting an arbitrage position with one of these deals is very easy; we simply buy a share in Company B for $55 and wait till the deal closes. When it closes we will exchange our Company B share for $57 worth of Company A's shares, which we can then turn around and sell in the stock market.

We should note that deals like this create the possibility of the dominant company issuing fractional shares, which it can't do because there is no active market for 1/10th of a single share of a company. To solve this problem the merger agreement carries a provision that cash will be tendered instead of fractional shares. As an example: in the merger agreement, Company A is to exchange $60 worth of its stock for each share of Company B's stock. At the time that the merger agreement was signed, $60 of Company A's stock equated to one share of Company A. But in the time that expired from the signing of the deal to the actual closing, Company A's stock went down in price to $50 a share. This means that at closing Company A will have to tender 1.2 shares of its stock for each share of Company B's stock to equal $60 ($50 x 1.2 = $60). Since Company A can't issue fractional shares, it will exchange one share of its stock, which is worth $50 a share, and $10 in cash for each share of Company B's stock.

In Summary

We have the stock-for-stock deal, the stock-and-cash-for-stock deal; and the cash-for-stock deal. The first two require locking in the price spread between the two companies' shares. The cash-for-stock deal just involves waiting for the deal to close and the check to arrive.

CHAPTER 10

Friendly Merger Arbitrage—Things Warren Considers When Determining the Probability of Completion

One of the major recurring problems that Warren confronts in the world of arbitrage and special investment situations is the probability of the merger completion. This is why he never buys on rumors. He prefers a sure deal, and the first step to making sure that it is a sure deal is only taking positions in mergers that have been publicly announced.

Now, even after the intention to merge has been publicly announced, and even if the merger is a friendly one, all kinds of things can still go wrong. There is the possibility that the deal might not be approved by a governing regulatory agency like the FTC, or it might not meet the approval of the antitrust people. There is the problem of shareholder approval; in many situations the company being acquired needs to have shareholder approval before it can merge. And if the dominant/acquiring company is issuing new stock to do the deal, it too will often need its shareholders to approve the issuance of new shares.

These and many other things can complicate Warren's sure thing. So in weighing the probability of success after the deal has been announced, it is good to review a few of the variables that Warren looks at in determining the probability of the deal succeeding. And the very first place he looks is the nature of the company making the offer.

The Nature of the Company Making the Offer

In the arbitrage world of mergers and acquisitions there are two kinds of buyers—strategic buyers and financial buyers—and they have very different track records on closing the deals they put together. So, in the art of determining the probability of success, it is important to understand the nature of these two classes of buyers and what they mean to us as arbitrageurs.

Strategic Buyers

These are companies that are adding to their existing business model. They grow by making acquisitions. They are usually, but not always, in the same or similar industry as the seller, and they are buying to expand their operations.

Strategic buyers are usually much larger than the companies they are buying. They are also often self-financing the deal and are paying in cash, so they don't have to finance the purchase by going to their bank and borrowing money. Think of IBM buying a smaller software company, or the giant food company Kraft buying Cadbury, the chocolate maker; or the financial powerhouse Berkshire buying BNSF, America's second largest railroad. In a friendly merger, once one of these super businesses has signed the deal, it is almost certain to go through regardless of the economic climate. It is interesting to note that even in the extreme economic environment of the last three years, we have seen Mars, Inc., acquire the Wrigley Company for $23 billion, the Dow Chemical Company acquire the Rhom and Haas Company for $15.3 billion, Kraft acquire Cadbury for $19 billion, and Berkshire acquire BNSF for $26.3 billion. These mega-deals got done in the middle of a deep recession.

As a rule, Warren likes it when the buyer is a strategic buyer, and the bigger the strategic buyer, the better.

Financial Buyers

These are the private equity and leverage buyout firms, which use lots of borrowed money to buy a company solely for the purpose of taking it private and then, in four or five years, taking it public again. The risk with these buyers is that they are relying heavily on borrowed money to get the deal done. In stable economic times these deals are usually safe bets. But in unstable economic times, when there is turmoil in the credit markets, these deals can potentially see their financing fall through in the blink of an eye. (Note: Warren is especially wary of deals that are contingent on finding "satisfactory financing" because this provides an easy out for the buyer to dump the deal.)

As a rule Warren tends to be more leery of financial buyers. He is particularly skeptical of them in an unstable economic environment. If we do bet on a financial buyer, we should stay with companies that have a solid track record of performing.

FINANCING AND THE ECONOMIC ENVIRONMENT

Once the friendly merger is announced and Warren has identified the nature of the buyer, he then shifts over to reviewing the economics of the deal and the economic environment we are in. He has a preference for betting on large strategic buyers who are self-financing the deal. If they're not self-financing, he is always interested in how they are going to acquire the money. If it is a cash deal, do they have enough on their balance sheet to do the deal or are they going to have to borrow the money or sell something to get it? A deal that relies on borrowed money or selling an existing asset has an added element of risk to it. If it is a stock-for-stock deal, the chances of the deal going through are far greater, but depend largely on the stability of the buyer's and seller's shares; so a

dramatic increase or decrease in share prices of either company could kill a deal even after the ink has dried on it.

Warren is also very interested in the economic environment. If the economy is stable and the credit markets are calm, and banks are busy financing mergers and acquisitions, it is much safer to do arbitrage deals than in an unstable economic environment where the banks aren't lending. This is particularly true for financial buyers who must rely almost entirely on borrowed money, either from their investors or from the banks.

MANAGEMENT OF THE SUBDOMINANT COMPANY

When Warren is ascertaining the likelihood of the deal being completed, he also likes to look at the intentions of the management of the subdominant company, the one being bought. Was management actively out shopping the company before there was a deal? Or was it one of those one-off deals, where if the buyer walks away there might not be another one for a long time?

When management is out shopping the company, it can be assumed that the majority of the board of directors are behind the idea of selling the company, and if their buyer backs out, it is safe to say that management and the board will be very motivated to go out and find another. This is

important in that it reduces the risk of the selling company's stock price dropping dramatically if the buyer walks away. A motivated seller is a good thing if you have an arbitrage position in the company.

Board Approval

If there is a merger, spin-off, reorganization, or liquidation, it will have to be approved by the board of directors of both companies. With friendly mergers, spin-offs, reorganizations, and liquidations, the board of directors has already approved the move by the time the company has made the announcement to the investing public.

In some cases, not only must the selling company's board approve the sale, the company's shareholders must approve it as well.

Shareholder Approval

Under Delaware corporations law, shareholders must approve all transactions that fundamentally change the nature of the corporation. The three basic types of fundamentally changing transactions are dissolution, merger, and the sale of substantially all of the company's assets. Since most publicly traded

companies in America are incorporated in Delaware, it is safe to say that any dissolution, merger, or sale of substantially all of the company's assets is going to require shareholder approval.

Determining the odds of getting shareholder approval and the deal closing, with a friendly merger or even the most hostile of takeovers, depends a great deal on who already owns the stock of the company.

If management owns large blocks of the stock and is behind the deal, as in a management-led buyout, there is a very strong likelihood that shareholders will approve the deal. The same thing applies to a company controlled by a single family, like the Sulzberger family, which controls the *New York Times*. If the Sulzberger family wants the *Times* to be sold, it's going to be sold. And if they don't want it to be sold, it is not going to be sold, no matter how high the bid.

If management owns very little of the stock and the vast majority of the shares are held by individual investors and/or mutual funds, and the offer is fair, there is a very good chance that the deal will happen if management is behind it. Institutional shareholders like a quick return and for the most part lack any long-term holding strategy. Anything that improves their quarterly results will make them smile.

For any deal that involves getting shareholders' approval, it is a good idea to find out just who the big shareholders are. For most of Warren's career, determining who actually owns and controls a company has been a difficult task, involving hours of research, digging through countless Securities and Exchange Commission (SEC) documents found in the basement of some library, or sending away for them from the company or a service that caters to investors. But in the age of the Internet, all the information we need to make informed decisions is just a few clicks away. Today, in just a matter of minutes, we can find out who the big shareholders are for almost any publicly traded company, and we can find out the last time they bought or sold any of their shares. Even the key managers' ownership positions are posted. The financial pages of Google, MSN, and Yahoo! all cover key owners and their positions.

For the arbitrageur in search of financial information it has become a wonderful world.

PROXY STATEMENT

If a shareholder vote is required it is done at a shareholder meeting. There are two kinds of shareholder meetings: (1) the "annual meeting," where the board of directors is elected and where the general business of the corporation is handled, which requires shareholder approval; and (2) "special meetings," where issues are handled that require shareholder approval that can't wait till the annual meeting. Though shareholders can go to the meetings and vote in person, most stay home and vote via a proxy card, using the telephone, and now on the Internet.

A proxy statement for voting on a merger is filed with the SEC and is sent to shareholders. The statement lists all the particulars of the merger; everything a shareholder would want to know to make an informed decision on how to vote, including the terms of the deal; and the date of closing.

A proxy, by its very nature, is a way to solicit shareholders' votes. And it does this by legally acting as an assignment of the shareholders' vote. Shareholders are asked to vote for or against the merger by checking a little box on the proxy card and then they assign their vote to a third party who will go the meeting and vote the shareholders' vote. Thus: voting "by proxy."

If there is a friendly merger, the seller must have a shareholder meeting in which the shareholders will vote on the merger. What is of key interest to us are the chances that the merger will get shareholder approval. If there is no major shareholder opposition, it is very likely that the merger will be approved. Shareholders are for the most part very short-sighted in their thirst for profits and will jump at any chance to get a 10% gain to their fortunes. It takes a very loud, major shareholder to get them to wait. If there isn't someone screaming that the deal shouldn't be done, the deal, more than likely, will get done. And if the dissenting shareholder isn't a majority stockholder, the deal will, more than likely, get done. It's that quick buck that usually seals the deal.

The deals you have to watch out for are the ones where there are major shareholders standing in the way. This can be lethal to any deal and greatly diminish the probability of success that Warren is looking for.

Department of Justice and Federal Trade Commission Approval

In the United States, antitrust issues are handled by the Department of Justice (DOJ) and the Federal Trade Commission (FTC). These two government entities have the power to review any and all mergers, friendly and hostile, of any size for possible antitrust violations. Which means they have the power to keep our deal from happening.

When the DOJ or the FTC decides to review an announced buyout or merger, they notify the companies and the general public of their intentions. Review of a buyout or merger by the DOJ can take a year or longer before being completed. This can be a serious detriment to the time value of the money aspect of Warren's arbitrage plays. A 10% return on his investment within six months is a pretty good deal, but if the DOJ or the FTC holds up the deal for a year or two, the attractiveness of a 10% return starts to diminish.

Plus, there is the added risk that the reviewing agency won't approve the deal and Warren's arbitrage play will fall apart. The only good part of this is that once a deal is announced to the public, both of these governmental agencies are quick to take action. Also, a company that is planning to buy another company can make a formal request to the DOJ or FTC for a business review of the proposed merger or acquisition. And though the DOJ and FTC do not give out advisory letters, they will state their enforcement intentions regarding the proposed merger of the two companies.

From the standpoint of predictability of a friendly or hostile merger, if the DOJ or the FTC announces that it is reviewing the merger or acquisition, it is safer to sit on the sidelines until they have made their ruling. Otherwise our money could be tied up for years waiting for their decision, and there is always the risk that they could kill the deal completely, which could result in our losing money instead of making money. Which is never a good idea.

A Competing Buyer Shows Up

The big bonus in the arbitrage game is when a competing buyer shows up. If there is more than one buyer and they are bidding against each other, it greatly increases the likelihood that the deal will get done. Because there is competitive bidding going on, it becomes very hard for anyone to say that the winning bid wasn't the best price. It can be argued that a competing buyer almost ensures that the highest possible price will be paid. A competing buyer adds to the "certainty" of the deal being done. So smile when one shows up.

In Summary

Friendly mergers are the most "certain" of all Warren's arbitrage investments: while they have a very high completion rate, there are still a number of things that can cause them to go astray. Such things as the nature of the buyer, financing, the economic environment, regulatory approval, and shareholder approval all present potential problems for even the best-laid plans. That's why it is good to know what these potential problems are, and to be able to weigh them into our risk evaluation of the merger to determine its probability of success.

CHAPTER 11

A Friendly Merger Arbitrage Case Study: Berkshire's Merger with BNSF

When Warren decided he wanted to buy the Burlington Northern Santa Fe Railroad he offered them $100 a share in either all cash or all stock within certain parameters. Let's look at the terms of the deal announced in the press on November 3, 2009, by the BNSF and Berkshire Hathaway:

TERMS OF THE TRANSACTION

The definitive agreement provides that each share of BNSF common stock will at the election of the shareholder be converted into the right to receive either (i) a cash payment of $100.00 or (ii) a variable number of shares of Berkshire Hathaway Class A or Class B common stock, subject to proration if the elections do not equal approximately 60 percent in cash and 40 percent in stock. The stock component of the consideration is subject to a "collar" whereby the value of each Berkshire Hathaway share received is fixed at $100.00 if the price of Berkshire Hathaway Class

A stock at closing is between approximately $80,000.00 and approximately $125,000.00 per share. If the value of Berkshire Hathaway Class A stock is outside of this collar range at closing, then the number of shares received of Berkshire Hathaway Class A stock will be fixed at either 0.001253489 per BNSF share for values below the collar range, or 0.000802233 per BNSF share for values above the collar range. The shareholder may receive Class A or, in lieu of fractional Class A shares, equivalent economic value of Class B Berkshire Hathaway shares, subject to certain limitations as described in the definitive agreement.

The transaction requires approval by holders of two-thirds of BNSF's outstanding shares (other than shares held by Berkshire Hathaway), and customary closing conditions, including Department of Justice review. Closing is expected to occur during the first quarter of 2010.

So the Berkshire-BNSF announcement gives us the terms of the deal and its approximate closing time, sometime in the first quarter of 2010, which means sometime before March 31, 2010. Under the terms of the deal BNSF shareholders will get either $100 a share in cash or $100 a share in Berkshire stock at the closing date. It has a collar attached to it on the upside—which protects BNSF from getting less stock if Berkshire's shares soar above $125,000 a share. And it has a collar attached to it on the downside—which protects Berkshire from having to cough up more of the company if for some unforeseeable reason Berkshire's shares were to get slammed into the floor.

The chances of the deal going through were very high. Both the dominant and subdominant companies agreed on the transaction. And Berkshire definitely has the money to complete the deal. Since Berkshire is an insurance company, there are no potential antitrust problems in merging with a railroad. The deal is about as bombproof as arbitrage opportunities get.

A check of BNSF's stock price on November 3, 4, and 5, 2010, tells us that we could have bought about as much as we wanted at approximately $97 a share (and about 64 million shares did trade at that price in that three-day period).

The arbitrage play would be to buy BNSF at $97 a share and take the $100 a share in cash or Berkshire stock when the deal closed in five months, which would give us a return of just slightly better than 3%.

But if we adjust it to an annual rate of return—3% divided by 5, and then multiplied by 12—we get an adjusted annual rate of return of 7.2%. Since one-year U.S. Treasury bills were paying less than 1% during that time period, the return on our arbitrage deal looked astronomically good. And as it turned out, the deal ended up closing in about 3.5 months, which means the adjusted annual rate of return was more in the neighborhood of 10.2%.

Now consider this: if we had borrowed money at an annual rate of 6%, which equates to a monthly rate of 0.5 of 1%, and had held the money for our projected five months till close, our projected borrowing costs would have been 2.5% (6% divided by 12, and then multiplied by 5, which equals 2.5%).

This means that we could have borrowed $1 million at a projected cost of 2.5%, or $25,000. If we took that $1 million and bought BNSF stock at $97 a share, we would have bought approximately 10,309 shares. With Berkshire promising $100 a share at closing, we could count on a profit of $3 a share, which equates to a total profit on our 10,309 shares of $30,927. Which means that on the $1 million borrowed and invested, our return would also be $30,937, which equates to a return of slightly better than 3% ($30,927 ÷ $1,000,000 = 3.09%).

But watch this: our actual out-of-pocket cost on the investment wasn't $1 million; it was our interest costs on borrowing the $1 million, which was projected to be 2.5% for the five-month period, which equates to $25,000 in interest charges.

A return of $30,927 on an investment of $25,000 equates to a profit of $5,927, which equates to a return of 23% on our money for the five-month period ($5,927 ÷ $25,000 = 23%), which adjusts to an annual rate of return of 55%

(23% divided by 5, and then multiplied by 12, which equals 55%). Leverage is like adding rocket fuel to our investment; we just have to make sure that the rocket is pointed in the right direction.

In Summary

The large number of friendly merger deals that present themselves in any given year makes them the largest class of potential arbitrage investments. Because both parties are agreeing to the deal, they have a very high level of "certainty" of completion, which is what Warren is looking for in an arbitrage opportunity, as it ensures his profit. As such, they present to us our greatest opportunity to profit as well.

CHAPTER 12

Acquisitions—the Hostile Takeover—the Most Dangerous Place Warren Goes to Make Money

Friendly mergers vastly outnumber hostile takeovers, on average, in any given year, to the tune of about 30 to 1. So the odds of our arbitraging a hostile takeover are rather small—the opportunities just aren't there. And Warren much prefers arbitraging friendly mergers in that there is greater certainty with them. Still, he has invested in a number of hostile takeovers over the years, and when he has done so, he has gone after them in a very big way. So it is appropriate that we spend a bit of time studying this very interesting and volatile area of arbitrage.

THE HOSTILE TAKEOVER

In a hostile takeover the potential Buyer—a company, leveraged buyout or private equity firm, or other entity—makes an offer to buy another company, which we will call the

Target company. The takeover is termed "hostile" because it is against the wishes of the Target company's board of directors. The process usually starts with the Buyer making a behind-the-scenes offer to enter into negotiations to buy the Target. The Target's board turns down the offer and the potential Buyer then goes around the Target's board by directly soliciting the Target company's shareholders with a direct offer to buy their shares. Once a majority of the Target's shares are purchased, the Buyer can take control of the Target's board and effectively take control of the company.

Understand, a potential Buyer only has three avenues to taking over the Target company.

1. It can get the Target company's board to approve the deal. If this happens, it becomes a friendly merger.
2. It can get a majority of the Target company's shareholders to go along with the deal, which means the Target company's shareholders can use their power to replace the board to force it to take the offer.
3. Or it can go into the market and buy the shares and then replace the Target company's board itself and in effect take control of the Target.

Both 2 and 3 go against the wishes of the Target's board and both will involve a proxy fight.

A proxy fight is a battle between the two groups of share-holders—one group supports the Buyer and is for the buyout, while the other group is supporting the Target's board and is against it. Though in theory a proxy fight can erupt any-time shareholders are voting on something, with mergers they occur during the Target company's shareholders' meeting to vote on the merger or election of a new board of directors. The reason for the proxy fight is that only a small number of shareholders ever show up to a shareholders' meeting, so the actual voting battle takes place via shareholder proxy state-ments. Thus, the name "proxy fight."

From Warren's perspective, proxy fights bring a great deal of uncertainty to the event. As such, they take much more analysis than your normal deal, where both sides agree.

While the financial press usually makes a lot of noise about a prospective fight, fights seldom actually occur. What usually happens is that the potential Buyer will start the fight because it is the only way to get around the Target's board. If the potential Buyer can't find the votes to take control, it will drop it, but if the Buyer can find the votes, it will go forward. The board of directors of the Target company will keep an eye on the situation, and if they see that they are going to lose, they will capitulate before the meeting. Most proxy fights end before they actually get to the voting stage, because nobody wants to spend the time and money fighting a losing battle.

However, every year we will see a few very vicious proxy fights that are conducted in the public arena of the press. In those cases it is best for us to sit out the fight and wait for the results. Remember, certainty of the deal being completed is the key to Warren's success in the field of arbitrage, and certainty does not exist in the middle of a proxy fight where neither side is budging.

ANNOUNCEMENT OF THE TENDER OFFER

An actual hostile takeover kicks off with what is called a tender offer, where the potential Buyer tenders an offer to buy all the shares of the company it wants to take over. It is usually announced with an ad in the financial press or a public announcement covered by the press. The tender offer is for all, or a controlling portion, of the Target company's stock. The offer is at a fixed price in excess of what the Target company's stock was trading at the day before, usually about 20% above, which leaves room for the Buyer to bump up the offer if it can't get the Target's shareholders to go along with the deal.

So, as an example, the announcement is made of a tender offer of $50 a share on a stock that was trading the day before at $38 a share. What happens next is where Warren makes his money. The stock price will rise to reflect that tender offer, but it will not match it. Instead the market will start to factor in the risk of the deal not being done and the time value of money, which might leave a price spread of as much as a few dollars. On a $50 offer, the stock might trade at a risk-discounted price of $45 a share. That leaves a $5-a-share profit to be made by Warren if he buys it at an after-announcement offer of $45 a share.

As the deal starts looking like it might really happen, the stock price will start to rise, up to, say, $49 a share. But if the deal looks like it might not go through, the share price will drop down, possibly to the low $40s and maybe even all the way back to $38 a share.

If another bidder shows up, it is possible that the second bidder will cause the Target company's shares to rise in price up to, and even past, the original tender offer. Even the rumor that another bidder might show up will send the price up.

If a large dissenting shareholder shows up, the Target's stock price will more than likely drop.

The trick, of course, is figuring out whether or not the deal is going to go through, and there are all kinds of variables that influence the "certainty" of the deal. So for the next couple of pages we would like to discuss some of those variables and their positive and negative influence on the Buyer being successful in their hostile attempt to take over the Target company.

Public Announcement

A hostile takeover is usually kicked off by an announcement to the public that the potential Buyer is offering to buy all the stock of the Target company. Normally Warren is waiting for the public announcement of the buyout. However, here the situation is not one of announcing an agreement between two willing parties, but rather giving public notice of a fight between two combatants.

From a probability of completion perspective, these situations are far more dicey than when the Target company has actively been seeking a buyer and has finally found one. In a hostile takeover the management/board of directors of the Target is actively fighting against being taken over. This, of course, greatly increases the chances of the buyout not occurring.

Single Controlling Shareholder

Companies that are controlled by a single or organized group of a few shareholders are almost never the target of a hostile takeover because a single controlling shareholder can kill the deal in an instant. If the majority shareholder is against the takeover, there isn't much a potential Buyer can do.

Hershey Foods Corporation is the perfect example of this phenomenon. This hundred-plus-year-old chocolate company is controlled by the Milton Hershey Charitable Trust, whose sole purpose is to support a home for twelve hundred orphans. Any attempt by a potential Buyer to take over Hershey Foods is usually rebuffed by the controlling Hershey Trust. That doesn't mean that Hershey's hasn't had its share of suitors over the years. It's just that the board of the trust has always voted them down. And once an attempt is voted down, there is no use going forward, since the Hershey Trust also controls the board of Hershey Foods.

Likewise, a single controlling shareholder that is "for" the buyout essentially ensures that the deal will be agreed to.

Large Number of Shareholders

Target companies are almost always controlled by a large number of institutional and individual shareholders. Most shareholders have a very short-term perspective, so they could easily be enticed to sell out by the 20% premium over the current market price. Also, the board of directors has a fiduciary duty to do what is in the best economic interests of the shareholders, and in these situations it is very hard for them to say no, especially if the offer is substantially above the Target company's average share price for the last thirty days.

BIDDING WAR

If the Target company is a business with predictable products—those that don't change over time, like brand name products that are producing a steady stream of earnings year after year—it is a sure bet that the Buyer's bid will attract other bidders, which means that a potential bidding war for the company might develop.

A bidding war for the Target is a good thing if we are holding an arbitrage position in the Target. A bidding war also means that, more likely than not, the Target company will be sold. If a bidding war develops it is very hard for the board of directors to make the argument that the high bidder's offering price is not adequate.

Warren set an arbitrage position on the 1988 RJR Nabisco buyout, anticipating that the company would attract a higher bid. He was comfortable doing this because the initial bid of $75 a share was by the management of the company, in what is called a management buyout—where the management of the company tries to buy the company from its shareholders. So the deal was certain to go through, in that management would never have put out a bid that it thought the board of directors would refuse. As luck would have it, the leverage buyout firm of Kohlberg, Kravis, Roberts & Co., also known at the time as KKR, showed up and made an offer of $90 a share. The bidding went back and forth between KKR and RJR's management until KKR finally won out with a bid of $109 a share. If we set our arbitrage position at $73 a share and sold it at $109 a share, it would have given us a return of 49%, on a profit of $36 a share, in about six short months. Which means our time-adjusted annual return on the deal would have been approximately 98%. This is why Warren so loves investing in arbitrage and other special situations.

HOSTILE TAKEOVER DEFENSES

Takeover defenses are one of the many things that can screw up a hostile takeover from being successful. These are strategies that the Target company can put into place before or after receiving the hostile offer. However, some of these takeover defenses actually end up helping us, in that they facilitate the company being sold. To assess the impact these takeover defenses have to the potential success of the hostile offer, whether they are good or bad for us, it is good to know what they are and how they work. So let's take a look at a number of the key takeover defenses, beginning with staggering the board of directors.

A Staggered Board of Directors

Believe it or not, the one thing that can screw up a hostile takeover more than anything else is to stagger the election of the Target's board of directors.

Boards of directors are usually elected en masse. This facilitates the hostile takeover. If the bidder can convince a majority of the shareholders of the Target company to go along with it, then the entire board can be removed with a single meeting. But with a staggered board, the directors are elected a few at a time, over a period of years. So even if the Buyer has the backing of a majority of the shareholders, it will still be impossible to take control of the board at the next shareholders' meeting. A study of ninety-three hostile takeovers found that if the Target company had a staggered board, it was half as likely to be taken over as the company that elected its board en masse. If you are looking at a hostile takeover and you see the Target company has a staggered board of directors, there is a good chance it will not be taken over.

Other effective hostile takeover defenses include:

Crown Jewel Defense: This is a strategy where the Target either sells or spins off its best assets in an effort to become less attractive as a target.

Flip-In Defense: Also known as the poison pill defense, this is a provision in the Target's corporate bylaws which gives the current shareholders of the Target company the right to acquire more of the Target's shares at a discount. The effect is to substantially dilute the per-share value of the company, which increases the cost to the hostile Buyer. It usually takes a court battle to get around this situation and it serves to make the Target unattractive.

Flip-Over Defense: Another type of poison pill defense. This one kicks in after the buyout and it gives shareholders the right to buy additional shares of the Target at a discount, after it has been acquired by the Buyer. The effect is to dilute the ownership of the hostile Buyer, and the value of its shares, which no company wants to have happen. Basically it says that if you try to take over the Target, it will destroy the value of your company's stock.

A Lobster Trap: This is where the Target firm says that no one with more than 10% of the firm's convertible securities—which can be converted into common stock of the company—can convert them. This means that you can buy all the convertible debt you want, but you can't convert it to common shares if you own over 10% of it. A Lobster Trap stops the hostile bidder from using the Target's convertible debt as a way to build a position in the Target. (Note: convertible securities— usually debt or preferred stock—are securities that can convert into another kind of security, usually common stock.)

A White or Gray Knight Defense: This is one of those defenses that actually help us. Here the Target company finds someone else to buy it, preferably a company that will treat the current management well after the takeover. The Gray Knight is just not as pleasing to the Target's management as the White Knight is.

Nancy Reagan Defense: (No, we're not joking.) Nancy, in a passionate plea to the spirited youth of America, urged them to "just say no" to drugs. In the world of takeovers the Target company always has the ability to just say no. It can always do this. But it had better have a good reason for doing so; otherwise angry shareholders will be suing. Honestly, this defense works about as well as Nancy's plea did with America's youth.

Pac-Man Defense: (Still not joking.) This is where the Target company turns around and makes a hostile offer for the potential Buyer. The term was coined by the late but great buyout king Bruce Wasserstein. (A moment of silence, please.) A perfect example of this was when Bendix Corporation tried to take over Martin Marietta Corporation. Martin Marietta turned around and made a bid for Bendix. To save itself, Bendix found a White Knight, Allied Corporation, and sold out to them instead of Martin Marietta. The Pac-Man defense does work.

In Summary

All hostile takeovers are filled with uncertainty, which is what Warren is trying to avoid. They present us with very little opportunity, because they make up only about 4% of all takeovers. This rarity of the event, and the even greater uncertainty of the hostile takeover being successful, almost always makes it safer to follow Nancy Reagan and just say no. We might even argue that from Warren's perspective, hostile takeovers should be avoided in their entirety. Still, in a few situations they can blossom into the perfect arbitrage play, especially if another Buyer shows up or if the Target company's management decides that it wants to join in the bidding. This can drive up the offering price well past the hostile bidder's original offer, which always makes us happy.

CHAPTER 13

Securities Buybacks/Self-Tender Offers—How Warren Arbitrages Them to Make Even More Money

Corporations often seek to buy back their own securities. Most often they are trying to buy back their common stock in an effort to shrink the number of shares outstanding, which decreases the equity in the business and, in theory, should cause an increase in the per-share earnings of the business— fewer shares outstanding means that the remaining shares get a bigger cut of the pie.

Sometimes corporations will buy back their common stock to help drive the stock's price up as a means to prevent or stop a hostile takeover.

Corporations also make offers to buy back their preferred stock, their convertible debt, debentures, and bonds in an effort to reduce their debt load or as part of a refinancing package.

When corporations decide to buy back their own securities there are several ways they can go about it. They can buy back the securities in the open market, which is okay if they are only after a small number of shares. But if they are after a large number, they run the risk of artificially driving the security's price up beyond what they were initially willing to pay for it.

To avoid the risks of an open market purchase, companies will often make a tender offer directly to existing shareholders. This lets the company get a lower price than if it were in the market slowly driving prices up, and it lets it avoid extreme general stock market fluctuations, which could also drive prices out of reach.

Tenders come in basically two forms: an offer at a fixed price; and an offer to buy via a Dutch auction. In both scenarios the current market price is lower than the price of the tender offer, which creates the arbitrage opportunity. Warren has been known to arbitrage both situations.

Offer at a Fixed Price

Here the company offers to buy x number of securities at a fixed price for a set duration of time. The stockholders will tender their securities and the company will keep buying shares until they have bought the number they have set out to buy. If too many of the securities are tendered, the company will often prorate the number they buy from each of the sellers. (As an example: you tendered 10,000 shares, but the shareholders' total tendered is 110% of the number of shares the company offered to buy. The company will then discount everyone's tender by approximately 10%, which means that the company will only buy 9,000 of your shares, the other 1,000 being returned to you.)

Arbitraging this situation is easy; we just subtract the current market price from the fixed price and determine your return within the time frame of the tender. The deal is absolutely certain to go through, so there is no risk there. The only risk is that the company will have too many securities tendered and we will be stuck with only a prorate share sold. This means that we will have to go into the market and sell the rest, which puts us at risk for downward market movement between the close of the tender and the time it takes to get rid of the rest of the position. However, with a common stock position it means that the leftover shares are probably worth more, in that there are fewer shares outstanding as a result of the buyback.

Offer to Purchase by Having a Dutch Auction

A company that wishes to buy a fixed dollar amount of its securities will often use what is called a Dutch auction. A Dutch auction is where the company sets up a low and a high price and then invites shareholders to tender shares between those two prices for a set period of time. The shareholders are essentially bidding between a set of numbers. The company then picks the lowest price between the low and the high in which it can buy back all the shares it intended to, and it offers that price to all the shareholders who tendered shares up to that price.

Arbitraging this situation is a bit more complicated than our fixed price offer. Here the problem is that the low price of the offer is usually the market price of the stock on the day before the company made its offer, and the current market price on the day after the announcement is usually higher than the low value. This means that if we are intent on arbitraging the situation, we will have to buy securities that are already trading in the range of value of the low and high price. Lucky for us that no one is going to tender their securities at a price below the current price. Which means our tendered stock will be tendered at a price closer to the high end than the low end.

To get a better idea of how a Dutch auction works, let's look at a recent Dutch auction that SonoSite, Inc., conducted to acquire $100 million worth of its stock.

Here is the public announcement:

BOTHELL, WA—January 11, 2010—SonoSite, Inc. (Nasdaq:SONO), the world leader and specialist in hand-carried ultrasound for the point-of-care, today announced that its Board of Directors has authorized SonoSite to repurchase up to $150 million of the Company's common stock or outstanding convertible notes for cash. In connection with the repurchase authorization, the Company will purchase up to $100 million of the Company's common stock through a modified "Dutch Auction" tender offer. SonoSite intends to commence the tender offer during the week of January 18, 2010.

Under the terms of the proposed tender offer, SonoSite shareholders will have the opportunity to tender some or all of their shares at a price within the range of $26.10 to $30.00 per share. Based on the number of shares tendered and the prices specified by the tendering shareholders, SonoSite will determine the lowest per share price within the range that will enable it to buy $100 million in shares, or such lesser number of shares that are properly tendered. All shares accepted for payment will be paid the same price, regardless of whether a shareholder tendered such shares at a lower price within the range. At the minimum price of $26.10 per share, SonoSite would repurchase a maximum of 3,831,417 shares, which represents approximately 22%

of SonoSite's currently outstanding common stock. Sono-Site will fund the repurchase from available cash on hand. The low and high ends of the price range represent approximately a 0% and 15% premium, respectively, to the most recent share closing price of $26.10 per share. Based on the January 8, 2010, closing price, the share price has increased 10% year-to-date.

The tender offer will be subject to various terms and conditions as will be described in offer materials that will be publicly filed and distributed to shareholders at the time of commencement of the tender offer during the week of January 18, 2010. Additional copies of the offer materials will also be available from the Information Agent, Georgeson Inc. The Dealer-Manager for the tender offer will be J.P. Morgan Securities Inc.

ARBITRAGE ANALYSIS

A look at the material from the Information Agent would have told us that the deal was set to close on February 18, 2010, or in about 1.5 months. We can also see that SonoSite is offering to buy up to 22% of its outstanding stock, at a 15% premium to the closing price of the company's stock the day before the announcement. Now, we can assume that a 15% premium to the closing price is probably not enough to attract 22% of the company's outstanding stock, so we can project that the price that SonoSite will have to pay will be the full $30, to attract as much of the stock that it can.

A check of the trading price of SonoSite the day after the announcement tells us that we could buy the stock for $28.22 a share. A purchase price of $28.22 a share against a selling price of $30 a share gives us a profit of $1.78 ($30 − $28.22 = $1.78) and a rate of return of 6.3% for the 1.5 months we would hold the investment ($1.78 ÷ $28.22 = 0.063). Adjusted to an annual basis, it equates to earning 50% a year. Given that U.S. Treasury bills for that period were paying under one half of 1 percent, our little SonoSite arbitrage is looking really good.

If we used leverage in the deal and borrowed the $28.22 at an annual rate of 7%, our interest costs would be approximately $0.25 per share for the 1.5 months we held the investment. Which means that our $1.78 profit would be reduced to $1.53 ($1.78 − $0.25 = $1.53). A return of $1.53 a share on a leveraged investment cost of $0.25 equates to a return of 612% for the 1.5 month period. Which is one heck of a return.

And how did our SonoSite do with its Dutch auction? Let's check out their press release on it:

SonoSite, Inc. (Nasdaq:SONO), the world leader and specialist in hand-carried ultrasound for the point-of-care, today announced the final results of its modified "Dutch Auction" tender offer which expired at 5:00 p.m. New York City time on February 19, 2010.

Based on the final count by the depositary, an aggregate of 2,960,350 shares of common stock were properly tendered and not withdrawn at prices at or below $30.00. Accordingly, pursuant to the terms of the Offer to Purchase, the Letter of Transmittal and applicable securities laws, SonoSite has accepted for purchase 2,960,350 shares of its common stock at a purchase price of $30.00 per share. These shares represent approximately 16.9% of the shares outstanding as of February 24, 2010. With the completion of the tender offer, SonoSite will have approximately 14,509,464 shares of common stock outstanding. The aggregate purchase price that will be paid by SonoSite in connection with the tender offer is $88,810,500, excluding transaction costs.

The depositary will promptly pay for the shares accepted for purchase.

So SonoSite didn't get the $100 million in stock that it set out to buy and ended up paying $88.8 million for 2.96

million shares, which equates to paying $30 a share. In a Dutch auction the company ends up paying the lowest price in its pricing spectrum that will attract all the stock it set out to buy. Here SonoSite set out to buy $100 million worth of its common stock, but it ended up only getting $88.8 million, which means that it will have to pay the maximum price in the pricing spectrum to all the shareholders who tendered.

In Summary

Corporate securities buybacks offer us a steady diet of arbitrage deals to invest in. What sets them apart from other deals is their high level of "certainty" of completion and the very short time they take to complete. Though the price spread is often quite small, the certainty of the deal and quickness of execution make them very attractive.

CHAPTER 14

How Warren Has Made Hundreds of Millions Investing in Corporate Reorganizations

CORPORATE REORGANIZATIONS

Warren has invested in many different types of corporate reorganizations over the years, but the two that he has favored the most have been reorganizations that converted the company from a corporate form of organization into either a royalty trust or a master limited partnership. Let's look at a couple of examples of these kinds of reorganizations and how Warren makes money off of them.

Businesses that have little or no long-term need for internal capital accumulation often find themselves in a position where they are distributing 100% of their net after-tax earnings. In such a situation the company that earns $1 a share pays corporate tax of approximately 34%, or $0.34 a share, and distributes the rest, $0.66, to the shareholders. It doesn't take a financial rocket scientist to see that if the company could avoid the corporate tax, it could pay out the whole

$1 to its shareholders, which would make its shareholders a whole lot happier.

Most companies have long-term capital needs that require them to retain a large portion of their earnings year after year, which means that they aren't in a position to pay out 100% of their net earnings. But the few companies that are have the option of reorganizing themselves into either royalty trusts or master limited partnerships. In both of these cases, these business entities don't have to pay any taxes on their net earnings if they pay them all out to their owners. These business entities offer a way for their owner/shareholders to avoid the punitive effects of a corporate tax on income.

Where Warren Makes His Money

Now, where Warren makes his money in reorganizations, from the corporate form to either a royalty trust or master limited partnership, is in the difference between the valuation the stock market gives the business as a corporation versus its future value as either a royalty trust or a master limited partnership.

What Warren has discovered is that a corporation that is paying out 100% of its after-tax earnings as a dividend will have its shares valued in relationship to what bonds are paying. As bond yields go up, the dividend payout is worth less and the price of the company's stock goes down. And, if bond yields go down, the company's payout is worth more and the price of the company's shares go up. Likewise, and this is a very important likewise, if the company's payout increases, the company's stock price will go up, just as if the payout decreases, the company's stock price will go down. If the company pays out more money, the company's shares are worth more money. And if the company reorganizes as either a royalty trust or a master limited partnership, it will be able to pay more money out, which means that its shares will be worth more money.

The buying opportunity that Warren exploits is this: after the company announces that it is going to convert into either a royalty trust or a master limited partnership, which means that its future dividend payout will increase after the conversion, the stock market won't recognize the increase until the conversion is completed and the dividend is actually increased and paid out. This creates a short period of time, between the announced reorganization and the actual date of the conversion, in which the company's shares are undervalued in relation to their future increase in value, due to the increase in the dividend payout that occurs after the conversion.

Why does this window of market inefficiency exist? These companies, because of their small market cap, are usually not well followed by Wall Street or the general public. Also, investors have a preference for valuing an interest-bearing security on the basis of what it is paying today, not what it might be paying tomorrow.

After the conversion to a royalty trust or a master limited partnership, the resulting higher dividend payout, in relationship to a low stock price, will draw the attention of Wall Street and the general investing public, which will drive up the price of the shares of these newly formed business entities.

To get a better idea of how to make money off of these special situations, let's look at a corporate reorganization into a royalty trust and a corporate reorganization into a master limited partnership that Warren invested in.

Tenneco Offshore's Reorganization into a Royalty Trust

In 1982, Tenneco Offshore Company, the owner of a partnership interest in a large pool of natural gas, was planning to reorganize itself and convert from corporate form to a royalty trust form to avoid corporate taxation. For every $1.21 that Tenneco was earning, it had to pay $0.41 in corporate income tax. That left $0.80 that could be paid out as a dividend to shareholders, who then had to pay personal income tax on it.

Tenneco's accountant and lawyers figured out that if Tenneco the corporation converted into a royalty trust it could avoid the punitive effects of the corporate tax and pay out its entire earnings to the new owners of the trust—who would be the old Tenneco's shareholders at the time of the conversion.

Warren and the rest of the world probably discovered Tenneco's management's intentions when it issued the following news release.

TENNECO OFFSHORE

HOUSTON, OCT. 20, 1982

The Tenneco Offshore Company said today that it is proposing to hold a special meeting of its stockholders before the end of the year to vote on a plan of dissolution. Offshore oil and gas properties in which Tenneco Offshore has a partnership interest would be transferred to a royalty trust and units of the trust would be distributed to stockholders. Tenneco Offshore, a publicly held company, is managed by the Telleco Oil Company, a unit of Tenneco Inc.

Once Warren was aware of the planned reorganization, all he had to do was wait until the stockholders approved it—which they did—before he started buying the stock.

Let's look at the economics of the transaction.

At the time of Tenneco's planned conversion from a corporation into a partnership, it owned a large pool of natural gas and was paying out to its shareholders 100% of proceeds of its net income from the sale of the gas. The company was paying out $0.80 a share a year as a dividend; with a market price for the company's shares at approximately $5.70 a share, this equates to an approximate annual rate of return of 14%. Since interest rates on Treasury bonds at that time were at an all-time high of 14%, the market was valuing the company at approximately $5.70 per share ($0.80 ÷ $5.70 = 14%).

As we said earlier, when Tenneco converted into a royalty trust, it could skip the corporate tax and pay out the whole $1.21 a share, which meant that the market should revalue the trust's shares upward to reflect their relative rate of return in regard to what they were paying before the company converted to a royalty trust, which is 14%. This meant that the company, after it converted, should see an increase in share price to approximately $8.64 a share ($1.21 ÷ 0.14 = $8.64).

The shortsighted stock market ignored the announcement that Tenneco was going to convert to a royalty trust and continued to trade its stock at $5.70 a share. Seeing this price discrepancy between the current market price and the after-conversion price, Warren started buying Tenneco shares.

After Tenneco made the conversion into a royalty trust, and increased its payout, the market revalued it upward to approximately $8 a share, giving Warren a potential profit on the trade of $2.30 a share ($8 − $5.70 = $2.30). And then Warren sold his shares, netting him a fast 40% return on a holding period of around a year.

We know the buying and selling dynamics of Warren's Tenneco trade. What we don't know for sure is whether Warren used leverage on this deal; if he did, he would have had to pay approximately 15% a year for the borrowed money (interest rates were really high that year). And he would have had to have the loan out for about a year. This equates to an interest cost of $0.85 a share on the deal ($5.70 x 0.15 = $0.85), which would have reduced his profit on the trade to $1.45 a share ($2.30 – $0.85 = $1.45). From a leverage standpoint, a return of $1.44 a share on an interest cost of $0.85 a share equates to a return of 170%.

The Tenneco deal was already a great investment without the use of leverage. But, as we have said before and will say again, the use of leverage on a for-sure arbitrage deal is the best way to really goose your return. And here it would have turned a great investment into a fantastic one.

SERVICEMASTER'S REORGANIZATION INTO A MASTER LIMITED PARTNERSHIP

Early in 1986 the ServiceMaster corporation, which was in the hospital and commercial cleaning business and owned Terminix pest control, was earning returns on equity of 50% or better. The company had little internal long-term capital needs and decided that it would be beneficial to its shareholders if it reorganized itself as a master limited partnership.

A master limited partnership offered ServiceMaster several advantages over the corporate form. The first was that if it converted into a master limited partnership, just like a royalty trust, it could avoid paying a corporate tax on its income if it distributed all of its net income to its shareholders. Second, any dividends that it paid out to its shareholders for tax purposes could be used to decrease the shareholders' cost basis in their shares. Which means that shareholders wouldn't have to pay any taxes on the distributions they received from ServiceMaster up to the amount they paid for their stock. They would, however, have a larger capital gain when they sold the shares, but up until then the distributions would have a tax-deferred characteristic to them.

The same stock market pricing dynamics that take place with a reorganization to a royalty trust also occur with a reorganization to a master limited partnership. In this case, in 1986, ServiceMaster had pretax earnings of approximately $0.70 a share and after corporate tax net earnings of approximately $0.44 a share, and it paid out a dividend of approximately $0.38 a share. After its conversion to a master limited partnership, it would be able to bump up its dividend to approximately $0.70 a share.

In the fall of 1986, ServiceMaster announced that at the

end of its fiscal year it would reorganize itself as a master limited partnership. At that time Warren started buying the company's stock, acquiring close to 5.1% of the company, or roughly 3.6 million shares, for approximately $9 share. With a 1986 dividend payout of $0.44 a share, and an average cost of $9 a share, Warren could calculate that the company was paying a return of 4.8%. He could also calculate that if the company made a payout of $0.70 a share, his return would increase to 7.7% a year.

Now, here is where it gets interesting: if the stock market maintained the relative value of the company in relationship to a pre-partnership return of 4.8%, Service-Master's share price would increase to approximately $14.58 a share (0.70 ÷ 0.048 = $14.58 a share). Which meant that Warren could calculate an increase in value of ServiceMaster stock to approximately $14.58 a share in 1987, the year following its reorganization into a master limited partnership.

In 1987, the year following the reorganization to a master limited partnership, ServiceMaster increased its payout to $0.68 a share and the stock market increased the price of its stock to $14.20 a share. This gave Warren a quick profit of $18.7 million on an investment of approximately $32.4 million. This equated to a 57% return on his initial investment, which he held for little better than a year.

In Summary

Reorganizations into a royalty trust or a master limited partnership offer Warren easy ways to make really good returns over a fairly short period of time. The converting company is usually one that doesn't need much in the way of new infusions of capital to stay in business, which means that it can pay out the vast majority of net earnings every year.

The beauty of this kind of special situation is that the stock market as a whole often ignores the reorganization until it is completed. This gives Warren plenty of time to invest in it. An added benefit is that there is little chance of the reorganization not happening once shareholders approve it. Certainty of the event equates to certainty of the profit, which allows Warren to commit large sums of capital with confidence.

CHAPTER 15

Corporate Liquidations—How Warren Turns Them into Liquid Gold

Sometimes a company is worth more dead than alive. Meaning that the assets of the business are worth more to the shareholders if they are sold off and the proceeds distributed to the shareholders than if the company continues on, operating as a business. This is different from spinning off a subsidiary from a parent company in that in a liquidation just the assets of the business are sold, not the managerial structure or the legal entity of the corporation itself. In a complete liquidation, where all the assets are sold, the company, as a legal entity, ceases to exist. In a partial liquidation, where just a portion of the company's assets are sold off, the company continues doing business, just in a smaller economic form.

In the United States, before 1986, a company could adopt a plan of liquidation that would allow it to liquidate its assets and send the proceeds to its shareholders without paying any corporate tax on the sale. It was a good way for management to unlock the hidden value of the company that the stock market was refusing to recognize. And in the world of special situations there was a great amount of this kind of activity in which Warren partook.

However, after 1986, the U.S. tax code changed and assets sold in a corporate plan of liquidation were henceforth taxed at the corporate level, killing this as a tax strategy for liquidating corporate assets. However, this strategy is still used to liquidate assets that are held in real estate trusts, allowing the trust to liquidate its property holdings and make a payout of the proceeds to the beneficiaries of a trust without the trust having to pay the equivalent of a corporate tax. When this happens, only the beneficiaries of the trust are faced with any tax liability.

As of today, in the United States, corporations have to pay taxes on any profit they have made selling their assets, and shareholders incur a potential tax liability when it is paid out to them. Trusts don't have to pay taxes on any profit from selling assets as long as the profits are distributed to the beneficiaries of the trust.

Now, as we said before, there are complete liquidations and partial liquidations, and there are voluntary and involuntary liquidations. Voluntary means the company freely decides to liquidate; involuntary means the company is forced to sell an asset, as when the government takes a piece of real estate by eminent domain proceedings, or in a corporate bankruptcy, where a company is forced to liquidate.

An area of liquidation that has drawn Warren's attention in the past has been the voluntary liquidation of real estate investment trusts.

LIQUIDATION OF REAL ESTATE INVESTMENT TRUSTS

Real Estate Investment Trusts are known as REITS in the investment world. Basically they are real estate investment companies that are set up as trusts, with the investors becoming beneficiaries of the trust when they invest in trust "units," which then go on to be publicly traded. The reason that they are set up as trusts is so that any income from rents or profit from the sale of real estate won't be taxed at the corporate or trust level; rents and profits that are passed through to the owners of the trust units are only taxed at the personal income level.

The business of a REIT is fairly simple: it sells the trust units and then takes the money and either buys or builds office buildings, shopping malls, and apartment buildings, which it then rents out to tenants. The net income from the rental operations is paid out to the owners of the trust units.

What happens, sometimes, is that the underlying value of the properties that the trust owns increases in excess of the market value that the trust units are trading at. As a simple example: X Trust's publicly traded units are trading at $25 a unit, but the liquidation value of X Trust's property equates to $33 a unit.

The reason for the unit's being undervalued relative to underlying property value is that REITs are usually priced in the market relative to what they pay out in yearly rent disbursements to the owners of the trust units. If rents go up, disbursements go up, and so does the price of the trust units. If rents go down, disbursements go down, and so does the price of the trust units. In fact, they are priced by the market a lot like bonds are, and the trust's rent payouts are seen as a kind of fluctuating interest payment, which adds an interest rate pricing dimension to the trading price of the trust's units. So if interest rates go up, the price of the units goes down, and if interest rates go down, the price of the units goes up.

Where Warren makes his money in the liquidation game is when the trust units are trading at a price that is below the liquidation value of the trust; the trust then decides to liquidate so that shareholders can realize the higher value, but the stock market ignores the event and continues trading the stock at pre-liquidation prices.

The sequence of events that usually happens is: the REIT decides to liquidate, to realize the full value of the underlying real estate, so it makes a public announcement that it is liquidating, but the stock market lags in adjusting the price of trust units upward to reflect the liquidation value. The lag exists because REITs tend to be small cap companies that the Wall Street analysts tend to ignore, and there is a certain amount of risk to the liquidation that needs to be evaluated, which takes time. But it is this lag in time that presents individual investors and Warren with an arbitrage opportunity. Let's look at an example.

MGI PROPERTIES LIQUIDATION

On August 12, 1998, the REIT, MGI Properties, made the following announcement in the financial press:

> MGI Properties announced today that its Board of Trustees approved a plan of complete liquidation and termination of the Trust (the "Plan") and directed that the Plan be submitted to the Trust's shareholders for approval. The Trust intends to submit the Plan to its shareholders for approval in October 1998.
>
> W. Pearce Coues, Chairman of the Board, stated that "management estimates that sales of the Trust's assets pursuant to the Plan will be made at prices that will yield aggregate net cash distributions of between $30 per share and $33 per share; however, no assurance can be given that per share net cash distributions will fall within such range." The timing of any distributions of such net cash proceeds will be affected by, among other things, the tim-

ing of sales of assets, income tax considerations and the establishment of reserves. Accordingly, no assurances can be made as to the actual amount or timing of such distributions, which could be made over a substantial period of time. The Plan and other pertinent information relating thereto will be set forth in the definitive proxy statement distributed to shareholders following its submission to the Securities and Exchange Commission and the Commission's review thereof.

Upon reading the above, Warren would have had five thoughts: (1) The reason MGI is liquidating is that the liquidation value of the underlying property value is in excess of the trading value of MGI's share price, or else the shareholders would never go along with it. (2) What is the trading price of MGI Properties' shares? (3) What is MGI Properties' per-share liquidation value? (4) What is the time frame of the liquidation? And last, but most important, (5) what is the likelihood of the liquidation actually taking place?

Is the market price of MGI's trust units below the estimated liquidation price? Warren knows from the above announcement that the estimated liquidation price is between $30 and $33 a share. A check of the market price of MGI's units puts them at $24 a share on the day of the announcement. This tells him that MGI's shareholders have a very strong financial reason to go along with the liquidation, which means that they will certainly approve of the planned liquidation. "Certainty" that a plan of liquidation will be executed is key to making money, because if it doesn't liquidate, we don't make any money.

This means that at $24 a share, Warren would be getting a projected return of between 25% and 37% on his investment. Which sounds great, but what is the time frame of the payout? A check of the documents that MGI filed with the SEC in connection with getting shareholder approval indicates that MGI plans to take two years to liquidate. Which would turn Warren's projected "annual" rate of return to somewhere between 12.5% and 18.5%. But there is an added bonus: while he waits for the liquidation, he would be receiving MGI's payouts from rents generated by the buildings, which in 1998 equated to approximately $1.22 a share. (But understand: as the liquidations occur, the rent payouts would diminish in relationship to the shrinking rent rolls.)

Warren ended up buying 1,141,300 shares of the trust, or 8.3% of all its outstanding shares. MGI ended up liquidating the majority of the property portfolio in 1999, and the rest in 2000, distributing approximately $30 a share, giving him a total return on his investment of approximately 25%. This equates to an annual rate of return of 12.5%. Which is a heck of a lot better than the 5% that U.S. Treasuries were paying back in 1998.

Okay. Let's run through the sequence for valuing liquidations.

1. We will first read about it in the financial press and then in documents filed with the SEC—which are available online and will tell us what the anticipated per-share liquidation value will be and the time frame in which the company intends to liquidate. We will also find out if there is the need for shareholder approval, and if that is required when the vote will occur.

   Anticipated Per-Share Liquidation value = _____
   Need of Shareholder Approval: Yes No
   Date of Shareholder Meeting _____

2. We then look up the trading price of the liquidating company and subtract the trading price from the liquidating price, which will give us our potential profit.

   Per-Share Liquidating Price _____
   Less Current Market Price _____
   Equals Potential Profit _____

3. The next thing we have to do is figure out the likelihood that the liquidation will occur. Here you have to keep up with the press and read all the documents that the company files with the SEC. But large discrepancies

in liquidation valuation and market price usually mean strong shareholder support for the liquidation. What we really have to watch out for is a single or group of powerful shareholders who will oppose the liquidation. With liquidations it is best to wait for shareholder approval; it is the only way that we can be certain that the liquidation will happen. Which goes back to Warren's strategy of waiting for the deal to be announced before investing in it. With liquidations we wait for the shareholders' vote of approval before making our investment.

The biggest danger with real estate liquidations is the great length of time it can take to sell off a number of properties. Unlike a tender offer, where there is a set date when the deal reaches fruition, a real estate liquidation can often take a number of years, increasing the chances that something will go astray. This usually means the property or properties don't get sold on schedule or at all. The saving grace is that even if the properties don't get sold, there isn't a great deal of downside risk, as long as the properties continue to be profitable and the real estate trust can continue its payouts to its shareholders. For quantifying the risk we would use the Graham arbitrage risk equation discussed in Chapter 5.

4. Then we need to figure out just how long it will take to accomplish the liquidation. A 25% return sounds

great, but if it takes five years, it knocks the return down to an annual rate of return of 5% a year. And a 3% return might not sound like much, but to earn 3% a month would require an investment earning an equivalent annual rate of return of 36%. In liquidations what seems small can really be large and what seems large can really be small; it all depends on how long the liquidation will take to occur.

Since most calculations of financial instruments that pay interest are quoted in yearly terms, it helps us as investors in liquidations to put our projected return into yearly terms. To figure this out, we take the projected rate of return, divide it by the length of time the liquidation will take in months, and then multiply our result by twelve. This gives the projected rate of return in terms of a yearly rate of return. Let's say your projected rate of return is 20% over a seventeen-month period. Take 20% and divide it by 17, which will give you a monthly rate of return of 1.176%. Multiply that by 12, the number of months in a year, which gives you a projected yearly rate of return of 14.1%. If the 14.1% a year looks attractive, you make your investment and wait for the liquidation to happen.

Before we leave this area of special situations we would like to look at one more liquidation in which Warren invested that in the end paid off far in excess of his expectations. This is the case of Warren's investment in Arcata.

Arcata Liquidation

Arcata was a paper and printing company and a major producer of redwood lumber that in 1981 was the target of the famed Wall Street takeover firm of KKR. At that time Arcata was litigating a dispute with the federal government over 10,700 acres of redwoods that the government took in 1978 for Redwood National Park. The government had offered to pay Arcata a total of $97 million for the property, but Arcata deemed that inadequate and sued for more compensation. The litigation looked as if it would take several years to be resolved. To convince Arcata shareholders to sell out, KKR offered them $37 a share and two-thirds of anything that the courts would award Arcata for the disputed redwoods.

The first question for Warren was whether or not the deal would go through. Here he said, "We had to ask ourselves what would happen if the KKR deal did fall through, and here we felt reasonably comfortable. Arcata's management and directors had been shopping the company for some time and were clearly determined to sell. If KKR went away, Acrata would likely find another buyer, though of course the price might be lower. Finally, we had to ask ourselves what the redwood claim might be worth. Your chairman, who can't tell an elm from an oak, had no trouble with that one: he coolly evaluated the claim at somewhere between zero and a whole lot."

KKR didn't back out of the deal and Warren bought 655,000 shares at an average price of approximately $34.90 a share, for a total investment of $22.8 million. As it turned out, KKR ended up paying $37.50 a share, which gave Warren an immediate profit of $1.7 million, for a 7.5% return on his investment, and since the payout happened six months from his initial investment, he could argue that it was the same as having an investment that paid an annual rate of return of 15%. And as a kicker, somewhere down the line, KKR would pay Warren two-thirds of the results of the redwood litigation.

That "somewhere down the line" occurred five years later when the court ordered that the federal government pay Arcata $519 million for the redwoods. KKR then paid Warren an additional $19.3 million, or $29.48 a share, for a total return of 91% on his initial investment.

Good things do happen to those who wait, and with liquidations, sometimes really great things happen to those who wait a little longer.

In Summary

Liquidations have historically given Warren very fertile ground to invest in. The three key elements are the value of the liquidation, the probability of its happening, and the time frame that it will happen in. While liquidations are few and far between, when they do occur, they can offer us some of the best profits in the arbitrage and special situations game.

CHAPTER 16

Corporate Spin-offs—How Warren Made a Fortune Investing in Them

One of the most lucrative special situations that Warren invests in are called spin-offs. Spin-offs are where a conglomerate that owns two or more companies feels that it would be advantageous to its shareholders' fortunes if it spins off one or more of its companies directly to its shareholders, with the company being spun off becoming a stand-alone publicly traded company owned by the same shareholders of the parent company.

Warren can make money when the conglomerate that is doing the spinning off is undervalued in the market relative to the underlying values of the companies that it owns. The company being spun off has the potential to trade at a higher price-to-earnings ratio than when it was tucked away inside the conglomerate. Warren buys shares in the conglomerate while it still owns the company that it is spinning off; then, after the company is spun off, he sells his shares in the conglomerate and keeps the shares in the company that was spun off. This buying sequence allows him to acquire at a bargain price the exceptional company that is being spun off.

Let's take a closer look.

THE REASON FOR THE SPIN-OFF

Corporations, as they grow, often acquire other corporations in very diverse businesses. As they acquire different companies they build into a conglomerate, which is basically a parent corporation, which owns many different subsidiary corporations.

Now, not all corporations are created equal; some have better inherent economics working in their favor, and the same is true of subsidiaries. Often a conglomerate is a collection of a few exceptional businesses coupled together with a dozen or more mediocre businesses. And when the stock market goes to value the conglomerate, it takes into account the collective economics of all the businesses that come under the umbrella of the parent corporation. Quite often this means that the stock market valuation tends to reflect the economics of the mediocre businesses more than it does the few exceptional businesses.

When this happens the management of the parent corporation, for the benefit of the shareholders, will try to unlock the value of the exceptional subsidiary with the great economics by separating it from the parent corporation and all its mediocre subsidiaries. The process of separating the exceptional subsidiary from the parent is called a spin-off. The exceptional business is spun off with the hope that the stock market will give it a higher valuation as a stand-alone company than when it was a subsidiary of the parent. Think hidden diamonds wrapped in ugly coal. When the coal comes off, all the world gets to see this beautiful diamond of a business, and people are willing to pay a lot more for diamonds than they are for coal.

Spin-offs are accomplished by having the parent company declare a tax-free spin-off. That happens under a pro-rate distribution, where shares of the company being spun off are sent to the parent company's shareholders in proportion to their existing ownership of the parent. As an example: if we owned 10% of the parent corporation, we would receive 10% of the subsidiary when it is spun off.

Corporate spin-offs come in two distinct flavors:

1. The publicly traded parent is trading at a lower price-to-earnings ratio than the subsidiary would be trading at if it were publicly traded. So the publicly traded parent spins off the subsidiary to its shareholders as a new publicly traded company, which in theory should trade at a higher price-to-earnings ratio, thereby unlocking the value of the subsidiary.

Warren is very interested in investing in this kind of spin-off, since it involves separating a business with better economics than the parent. He is especially interested when the subsidiary is a business with what Warren calls a durable competitive advantage that gives it exceptional economics. (We discuss how to identify a company with a durable competitive advantage in our books *The New Buffettology* and *Warren Buffett and the Interpretation of Financial Statements*.)

2. The other kind of spin-off is where a publicly traded parent wants to rid itself of some debt to improve its balance sheet, so it loads up a mediocre-performing subsidiary with debt and then spins it off. This frees the publicly traded parent of debt, which results in improving the economics of the parent's business and, hopefully, its stock price.

Warren is not interested in these situations because the company being spun off is basically a sacrificial cow, with its business economics being burdened with too much debt. It's hard for a company to grow if it is spending every dime it makes servicing debt.

The spin-off situation that Warren is most interested in is where the parent company is attempting to unlock the value of one of its subsidiaries with exceptional economics by spinning it off to its shareholders. A company with exceptional business economics, from Warren's perspective, offers him the greatest possible long-term investment gain. Being able to buy one at a discounted price is basically his dream investment—a great company, selling at a cheap price.

The reason for the discounted price is that few investment institutions—like mutual funds and brokerages—follow the economics of the "hidden business" that is being spun off. They follow the parent company, the one with the poorer economics. But when the exceptional company is finally spun off, it pops up squarely in the investing public's eye, and responding to the spun-off business's exceptional economics, they drive up its stock price.

FINDING THE SPIN-OFF

The place where you will first find out about a planned spin-off is in the financial news. The nature of the spin-off will be discussed as to whether it is a parent company dumping debt on a subsidiary, or a publicly traded parent trying to get its shareholders added value by spinning off a shiny subsidiary that will trade in the stock market at a higher valuation than its lumbering parent.

Dun & Bradstreet Corporation's decision to spin off Moody's Investors Services was first made public with a news release on December 16, 1999. The company announced that it was under considerable pressure from shareholders to do something about the value of its poorly performing stock, and in response had devised a plan where it would separate Moody's Investors Services—the bond-rating company—from Dun & Bradstreet's other operating companies, and in the process create two publicly traded concerns. The company went on to say that its investment bankers, Goldman Sachs, had made a presentation to the Dun & Bradstreet board of directors on the benefits of unlocking the true values of its individual business if it separated Moody's Investors Services out from all Dun & Bradstreet's other businesses. It also pointed out that while Moody's accounted for 53% of Dun & Bradstreet's net income, it only accounted for 27% of its total revenues and 10% of the work force, which tells us that Dun & Bradstreet was separating out its star business so Moody's would be able to shine.

DISCOVERING THE ECONOMICS OF THE BUSINESS BEING SPUN OFF

Once the company being spun off has been identified, we need to check up on the economics of its business. This is often hard to do, in that the economics of the business being spun off are often hidden within the company's general numbers reported in the company's annual report. However, there is a document that all companies file with the Securities and Exchange Commission, or SEC, called a 10k, which contains more information than the annual report and will often break down a conglomerate's income business by business. Also, the company will be making filings with the SEC concerning separation of the two businesses that will give some indication of the economics of the business being spun off.

A review of the SEC documents for Dun & Bradstreet in 1999 would have told Warren the following things about the economic nature of Moody's:

That Moody's was and is in the business of rating bonds and that it had 37% of the market, with Standard & Poor's holding 42%.

That Moody's had rated over $30 trillion of the world's debts.

That Moody's rated the debt of over a hundred countries.

That in 1999 Moody's had 4,200 corporate relationships.

That Moody's also had rated 68,000 public finance obligations.

That Moody's publishes thousands of pieces of credit research each year. Twenty-eight hundred companies throughout the world purchased its research on an annual basis, and there are over fifteen thousand individual users within those companies.

And that Moody's had been named the leading rating agency by *Institutional Investor* magazine for the past five years.

On the financial side Warren would have discovered that Moody's in 1999 had seen substantial revenue and operating income growth over the previous twenty years.

REVENUE ($ IN MILLIONS)

OPERATING INCOME ($ IN MILLIONS)

	1980	1981	1982	1983	1984	1985	1986
Revenue	29.3	32.2	41.5	46.7	56.7	80.6	108.4
Operating Income	17.7	19.6	25.1	25.9	31.3	47.2	61.8

	1987	1988	1989	1990	1991	1992	1993
Revenue	115.5	137.3	138.3	155.2	188.3	246.7	297.9
Operating Income	60.2	69.9	61.4	70.9	84.9	119.5	149.8

	1994	1995	1996	1997	1998	1999
Revenue	280.3	294.2	349.8	423.1	495.5	564.1
Operating Income	116.1	115.0	135.6	185.7	223.5	273.9

Moody's also had profit margins around 40%. Consistently strong earnings growth and high profit margins plus a strong market position for its products indicate that Moody's is a company with exceptional economics working in its favor, the kind of company that Warren likes to hold for the long term.

THE ACTUAL SPIN-OFF

Another thing that SEC documents can tell us are the dynamics of the spin-off, such as the new corporate structure, the date of the spin-off, and the number of shares in the new company shareholders will receive.

In the separation of Moody's from the rest of Dun & Bradstreet, the parent company retained the Moody's operation, changed its name to Moody's, and took the rest of Dun & Bradstreet's operations and dumped them into a newly formed corporate entity, giving it the old name Dun & Bradstreet. Shareholders of the old Dun & Bradstreet received new stock certificates with the Moody's name on it, representing ownership in Moody's, and they also received another new stock certificate with the name Dun & Bradstreet on it, representing ownership in the new Dun & Bradstreet. So, under the terms of the spin-off, if we owned a hundred shares of the old Dun & Bradstreet before the spin-off, after the spin-off we would own a hundred shares of Moody's (which is the old Dun and Bradstreet with a new name) and fifty shares of the new Dun & Bradstreet.

MANAGEMENT

When a company spins off its darling subsidiary with brilliant economics working in its favor, the old management usually likes to go with the company with the better economics. The company's top brass knows where the money is being made and likes to stay around it, so they naturally go with the star and leave the dog behind. It is also an easy way to tell which is the better company with the best long-term growth prospects. Just follow the top management; they know where the gold is.

Once a company announces that it is doing a spin-off, it must comply with a certain number of government requirements, including registering the new shares of the company with the SEC via the filing of a Form 10 Registration Statement and receiving from the IRS a ruling confirming that the new shares being distributed will be tax-free to the company and to its shareholders. Notice of these events and the particulars of the distribution are usually reported upon by the financial press, which tells investors that the company is serious about going through with the spin-off. See the example below.

Dun & Bradstreet Shareholders

The Dun & Bradstreet Corporation (NYSE:DNB) ("D&B" or "the Company") announced today that it has filed a Form 10 Registration Statement with the Securities and Exchange Commission in connection with the planned separation of D&B into two publicly traded companies. The Dun & Bradstreet Corporation ("New D&B") will consist of the Dun & Bradstreet operating company, the global source for instant, reliable business information. Moody's Corporation ("Moody's") will consist of Moody's Investors Service, Inc., a leading global credit rating, research and risk analysis firm.

D&B has received a ruling from the Internal Revenue Service that the distribution by the Company of shares of New D&B common stock will be tax-free to the Company and its shareholders for U.S. federal income tax purposes, except to the extent that cash is received in lieu of fractional shares of New D&B common stock.

The Company expects to complete the separation of the two businesses by the end of the third quarter of this year.

"The separation of Dun & Bradstreet into New D&B and Moody's will allow each company to pursue focused strategies appropriate for its specific business," said Clifford L. Alexander, Jr., chairman and chief executive officer of The Dun & Bradstreet Corporation, who will serve as non-executive chairman of Moody's following the spin-off. "In addition," Alexander said, "the separation will also enable investors to evaluate the respective businesses on a stand-alone basis and to participate directly in the potential of two separate companies."

In connection with the distribution, D&B will change its name to Moody's Corporation and New D&B will change its name to The Dun & Bradstreet Corporation. New D&B will retain the ticker symbol "DNB" on the New York Stock Exchange. Moody's will also list on the NYSE under a ticker symbol yet to be determined.

The separation will be accomplished through a spin-off of New D&B from the Company through the distribution of all of the outstanding shares of New D&B common stock to the Company's shareholders. This distribution will take the form of a dividend of one share of New D&B common stock for every two shares of the Company's common stock held on the record date.

How Did Warren Do?

During the last four months of 1999 and the first six months of 2000, Warren would increase Berkshire's stake in Dun & Bradstreet to 24 million shares, for $499 million, for an average price of $21 a share. The spin-off took place on September 30, 2000, which, under the terms of the spin-off, transformed his 24 million shares in Dun & Bradstreet into 24 million shares in Moody's and 12 million shares in the new Dun & Bradstreet.

Over the next three years, following the spin-off, Warren sold off his 12 million shares in the new Dun & Bradstreet, for an average price of approximately $30 a share, giving him back a total of $360 million. That reduced his cost basis in his 24-million share of Moody's stock to $139 million, or $5.56 a share ($499 Mil. – $360 Mil. = $141 Mil.).

Warren kept his Moody's stock and in 2005 it split 2 for 1, which meant that Berkshire now had 48 million shares of Moody's, which he kept till 2010, when he started selling it off at a pre-split equivalent price of $60 a share, which gave him an annual compounding rate of return on his initial investment of approximately 27%.

In Summary

Spin-offs are a way for Warren to buy exceptional businesses at bargain prices. However, both mediocre and exceptional businesses get spun off, so we have to be sure of the economic nature of the business being spun off before buying the stock of the parent; otherwise we may end up with the mediocre business instead of the exceptional one. As we said earlier, Warren's methods for identifying an exceptional business are discussed in great detail in our books *The New Buffettology* and *Warren Buffett and the Interpretation of Financial Statements*. We highly suggest reading both to learn more about investing in corporate spin-offs.

CHAPTER 17

Corporate Stubs—Where Warren Got His Start in Arbitrage

Corporate stubs is a funny name for a class of contingent or residual interests in a company. They come into being because of a merger, acquisition, liquidation, or reorganization. They have an assortment of formal names, including: minority interests, certificates of beneficial interests, certificates of participation, certificates of contingent interests, receipts, scrip, and liquidation certificates.

Though there are many different kinds of stubs, almost all of them can be classified into three basic categories. There is the fixed-asset stub, which is a discount situation against a cash claim. There is the participating asset stub, which is set to a minimum amount but has some upside potential as well. And there is the fluctuating asset stub, which is supported by a stated amount in property or securities that have the potential to fluctuate in value.

One of the earliest Warren arbitrage stories involves his arbitraging the difference between the market price of the company's shares and the value of the stubs they were being exchanged for. To get a better understanding of how stubs work, let's take a detailed look at this real-life example.

The Rockwood & Company Arbitrage

In 1954, Warren was a young analyst in New York City working for his mentor, Benjamin Graham. Graham had identified an arbitrage opportunity in a chocolate manufacturer and a cocoa wholesaler by the name of Rockwood & Company. Rockwood had found itself in an interesting situation: the price of cocoa had shot up from 5 cents to 50 cents a pound, giving Rockwood a potentially huge windfall profit on the large storehouse of cocoa beans it held. The problem was that if it sold the beans it would have to pay an income tax on the profit—one level of taxation—and then when it paid the money out to the shareholders as a dividend, they too would be taxed—a second level of taxation.

An enterprising Chicago businessman by the name of Jay Pritzker came to the rescue. After taking a controlling interest in Rockwood, Pritzker instigated a plan to get out of the cocoa business and use the cocoa beans to buy back its stock.

Pritzker had identified a provision in the U.S. tax code that allowed Rockwood to liquidate a part of the business and not be taxed on it on the gain. The proceeds to the shareholders would then be classed as a return on capital and taxed as a capital gain as opposed to ordinary income. The plan went like this: Rockwood would allocate the beans it wanted to sell to its subsidiary and then liquidate the subsidiary. The way Pritzker wanted to liquidate the subsidiary was to take the warehouse receipts (stubs) for the beans held by the subsidiary and swap them for the outstanding shares of the company's stock. This meant that if we owned Rockwood's stock back then, we could have swapped it tax-free in exchange for the cocoa warehouse receipts (stubs). Pritzker engineered it so that warehouse receipts (stubs) each held $36 worth of beans, which, with Rockwood's shares trading at $34 a share, created an arbitrage situation. Investors could buy the company's shares for $34 a share and trade them for the cocoa bean warehouse receipts (stubs) worth $36 apiece. Since there was a ready market for the cocoa bean warehouse receipts, the stubs could easily be converted into cash for a two-dollar profit within about two weeks' time. This equates to about a 6% rate of return, which on an annual basis equates to a yearly return of over 250%. It was a very attractive arbitrage deal.

Because the cocoa bean warehouse receipts didn't have to be sold and because they could fluctuate in value along with the price of cocoa beans, we would classify these stubs as the fluctuating asset kind. (Graham locked in the spread by shorting an equal amount of cocoa beans on the commodity exchange, which stopped him from participating in the upside if the price of cocoa beans shot up, but locked in his $2 profit if it went down. Remember, in Graham and Warren's world, arbitrage is all about certainty, and a certain $2 is infinitely better than a chance of great gain at the potential cost of great loss.)

Stubs Representing an Accrued Dividend Claim

Sometimes, in a reorganization, which results in a recapitalization, there will be stubs issued as a claim on unpaid cumulative preferred dividends that have accrued but haven't been paid. These kinds of stubs can trade in the over-the-counter market and usually trade at a deep discount until there is some indication that the company intends on making good on them. The reason that they are eventually made good is that the company can't pay out a regular dividend on its common stock until the stubs are paid off. These kinds of stubs come under the classification of fixed-asset claims, because the amount that the stub is worth is fixed on the amount of the dividends that have accrued but haven't been paid. Because of the underlying security, the cumulative preferred shares no longer exist; the dividends are no longer accruing. The stubs only represent the preferred dividends that haven't been paid, so it is a fixed amount.

Stubs for a Tax or Legal Claim in a Liquidation

Sometimes in a liquidation there are outstanding tax or legal claims left standing for years as they make their way through the courts. What usually happens is the government has taken property through its powers of eminent domain, but has offered too little in compensation to the company. Or there is an ongoing court case regarding a tax refund. Any of these events may be securitized and traded in the over-the-counter market. A stub of this nature would be one where it is set to a minimum amount—usually the rejected government's offer of compensation—and it would have the upside potential of a positive ruling from the court.

Leverage Buyout Use of Stubs

In the world of leverage buyouts, stubs represent a minority interest in the company being bought out. A private equity group or leveraged buyout firm will use debt to finance the buyout of a majority of the target company's shares, but instead of buying all the company's shares, it will often leave 10% to 15% of the company's publicly traded shares in the hands of the public. Often these stubs trade at deep discounts to the underlying value of the business. Arbitraging these kinds of stubs is not attractive to Warren, as there is usually no set date when the stub will trade at its full value relative to the value of the business. It's an open-ended investment that may or may not pay off, depending on the fortunes of the business. Warren is only interested in arbitrage situations that depend on some kind of corporate action to increase the value of his investment, regardless of how the underlying business performs.

In Summary

Stubs can take many different forms, and can make their appearance in many different types of arbitrage and special situations and under a dozen or more different names. For Warren they are where he got his start, and he has made serious money arbitraging stubs over the years.

CHAPTER 18

Where Warren Looks to Find the Golden Arbitrage Deals

Once upon a time, discovering what companies were planning on merging, attempting a hostile takeover, spinning off a business, doing a liquidation, planning a share buyback, or reorganizing into a trust or partnership required that we keep a vigilant eye on the financial press and any and all services that track such corporate events.

Today, as in the early years of Warren's career, the *Wall Street Journal* is the mainstay of investment research in discovering arbitrage opportunities. Warren also likes to read the major regional newspapers in his search for investment opportunities.

In the age of the Internet we are fortunate to have at our fingertips a vast array of research tools to help us discover potential arbitrage opportunities. For pay services there is mergerstat.com, which not only tracks mergers on a world scale, but will e-mail you notices of what is going on. The *Wall Street Journal* has paid services that track mergers as well.

On the free side you have the magical search engines at Yahoo!, which runs a great financial site that tracks mergers and acquisitions and can be found at http://finance.yahoo.com/news/category-m-a and http://us.biz.yahoo.com/topic/m-a/. Also, MSN tracks mergers and acquisitions on a world scale at http://news.moneycentral.msn.com/category/topics.aspx?topic=TOPIC_MERGERS_ACQUISITIONS.

For tracking tender offers, just Google the words "tender offer" and hit "news." All the large publicly announced corporate tender offers will show up. You can also Google "mergers" and hit "news" and read about the different mergers for free.

And we always like free.

CHAPTER 19

Tendering Our Shares—How Warren Cashes In

Taking a position in a merger, hostile takeover, or tender offer is easy: you just call your broker or go online and buy shares in the company that is being bought, being taken over, or is tendering for its own shares. That's simple enough.

But once we own shares we have to tender them to make any money, and we have to tender them within the window of the offer. We just can't sit around waiting for the money to come to us, we have to go get it, and if we don't, we just might not be able to cash in.

The company doing the buying will make an announcement that it is asking shareholders to tender their shares between, say, June 1, 2010, and June 20, 2010. This time period for tendering is usually between twenty and sixty days, and under certain circumstances the time period may be extended.

If we don't tender our shares within that window of time, all kinds of strange things can happen. We may be stuck with the shares and have to try selling them directly in the market.

Or we may end up with another fixed price at which the company will buy them from us. Either way it may not be as good a deal as the tender offer.

Once the buyout is made public there will be a formal request for us to tender our shares. It may come as a written notice, or we may just read about it online—a lot depends on how long we have owned the shares. If we already own the shares, we will most likely receive a recommendation/solicitation to purchase, which has been filed as a Schedule 14D-9 with the SEC. This gets into the nitty-gritty of why it is a good idea to sell our shares. We will also receive a written offer to purchase, which is part of the Schedule TO (TO stands for tender offer), which is also filed with the SEC. Since we probably didn't own shares in the company until after the announcement of the event, we will probably have to go online to the SEC EDGAR filing system and do a search for the company's name, which will take us to the Schedule 14D-9, the Schedule TO, and the Offer to Purchase. It's here we will really learn about the particulars of the deal and when and where to tender our shares from these documents.

Since we more than likely bought our shares through an online brokerage like Charles Schwab or TD AMERITRADE, which continue to hold our shares for us, we will have to call them and give them instructions to tender our shares. It is very important to call them and tell them to tender your shares, because if you don't, they won't be tendered.

Since the tendered shares aren't technically being sold, we usually don't have to pay a commission. Some firms, however, will charge us a service fee of between $30 and $50 on the entire transaction. But even this fee is often waived if we do enough trading with the firm or we have a large enough account with them.

We should note that sometimes in a merger you don't have to do anything if you hold the shares with your brokerage firm, especially in a share-for-share deal where our old shares are simply exchanged for new shares. But if you are holding the actual paper stock certificates, then you will have to tender them to get in on the exchange.

The best thing to do is to hold the shares with the online brokerage house. The folks at the discount brokerage Charles Schwab will send us timely e-mail notices of when we have to tender. They will also send us an e-mail that gives us the convenience of doing the tender online. Just click a few icons, type in the number of shares you want to tender, and click another icon and the tender is done. What could be easier? And if we want to we can still phone Schwab and have a broker personally handle it.

WITHDRAWING SHARES FROM BEING TENDERED

During the time period to tender our shares, we also have the right to untender them—after we tender our shares we may decide not to wait until the tender to sell them, or we may decide we want to hold the shares for the long term. Whatever the reason, once tendered, they can be untendered during the window for tendering. As an example: let's say that the window for tendering is between June 1, 2011, and July 31, 2011, and we tender our shares on June 2, 2011. We then have until July 30, 2011, to untender our shares. (The actual procedural dynamics on this can vary from brokerage house to brokerage house, so we need to inquire from our brokerage when the last day is that we can untender our shares.)

If the tender offer is increased in price after we have tendered our shares, we automatically receive the increased price for our shares. Which always makes us happy.

In Summary

To make our money we have to tender our shares within the time period designated in the tender offer, which can be found online in the SEC filing system. The online brokerage houses like Schwab make this easy to do with timely e-mails and online tendering.

In Closing

Thank you for taking this journey with us into the fascinating world of *Warren Buffett and the Art of Stock Arbitrage*. While there are a hundred more facets and subtleties that can show up in any arbitrage deal, you should now have enough information, skill sets, and investment tools to successfully begin navigating this very lucrative area of finance. In a year or two you may even find yourself with your own arbitrage and special situation investment operation.

If you have any questions, please feel free to write us. You won't always get a prompt reply, but we will eventually get back to you. Financial questions tend to get answered a lot faster than personal ones. To contact us, please write to: Marybuffettology@gmail.com or Davidbuffettology@gmail.com.

For speaking engagements please contact Simon & Schuster's Speakers Bureau at http://speakersbureau.simonandschuster.biz.

Best wishes and happy arbitraging!

MARY BUFFETT AND DAVID CLARK

Glossary of a Few Key Terms

Acquisition—When a company acquires another company, it is called making an acquisition.

Arbitrage—For our purposes the buying of a stock on one date and having an offer to sell it to someone else at a higher price on a future date.

Arbitrageurs—People who engage in arbitrage for a living.

Company with a durable competitive advantage—A company that has a product or line of products that don't change over time, that owns a piece of the consumer's mind, and that has superior long-term economics working in their favor. Often it is a consumer products company, but there are many exceptions, especially in the service industries. These are the kinds of companies that Warren loves to invest in for the long term.

Convertible debt—A bond or preferred shares that are convertible into the common stock of the company.

Debentures—In the U.S. an unsecured corporate bond. In the UK debentures are secured.

Dutch auction—A method of making a tender offer within a specific price range set by the company making the tender. However, a Dutch auction forces the party tendering the stock to name the price it will tender at. The buyer will then pay the lowest price possible in the set price range that will allow him to acquire all the shares he intended to buy.

Friendly merger—A merger in which both companies and their respective boards agree to the merger.

Hostile takeover—An unfriendly merger where the target company's board has refused to merge with the hostile raider and the raider has gone around the target's board directly to the shareholders of the target.

Leverage—Borrowed money. If we borrow money to buy stocks we are using leverage. In the UK it is called gearing.

Liquidations—A process of selling off the assets of the company.

Merger—When two companies join together and become a single company.

Merger agreement—The agreement between two merging companies that spells out the terms of the merger.

Proxy statement—Whenever a U.S. company is soliciting shareholder votes it must send out to its shareholders a proxy statement, which is also filed with the SEC as Form DEF 14A. The proxy statement will spell out the voting procedure and information, the background information on the company's board, the board's compensation, and the executive compensation.

Proxy voting—A procedure for delegating to another member of the voting body the right to vote an absent member's vote. The person assigning his vote is called the principle and the person receiving the assignment is called a proxy.

Reorganizations—For our purposes this is where a corporation reorganizes as either a royalty trust or a master limited partnership. It can also mean a company reorganizing its finances.

SEC—An abbreviation for the U.S. Securities and Exchange Commission, which is a federal agency that governs security transactions. Their domain includes mergers and acquisitions and any accompanying tender offers.

Self-tender offers—This is where a company buys back its own shares by making an offer to buy a large number of shares directly from its shareholders at either a fixed price or by a Dutch auction.

Spin-off—This is where a conglomerate spins off one of its many companies to its shareholders as a new publicly traded company.

Tender offer—An offer to buy a specific amount of a company's stock within a specific time period, either at a fixed price or by a Dutch auction.

Acknowledgments

We wish to thank our publisher and editor, Roz Lippel, and the rest of the staff at Scribner for doing such a wonderful job in the production of the book. They are the best in the business and we are grateful for the high level of professionalism they bring to this project.

INDEX